25 Bicycle Tours in Eastern Pennsylvania

Day Trips and Overnights from Philadelphia to the Highlands

Dale Adams and
Dale Speicher

SECOND REVISED EDITION

Backcountry Publications
The Countryman Press, Inc.
Woodstock, Vermont

For our parents, who watched us *not* outgrow our bicycles.

An invitation to the reader: Although it is unlikely that the roads you cycle on these tours will change much with time, some road signs, landmarks, and other items may. If you find that changes have occurred on these routes, please let us know so we may correct them in future editions. The authors and publisher also welcome other comments and suggestions. Address all correspondence:

Editor, Bicycle Tours
Backcountry Publications, Inc.
P.O. Box 175
Woodstock, Vermont 05091

© 1984, 1989 by Dale Adams and Dale Speicher
All rights reserved

Second edition: second printing, 1990
Published by Backcountry Publications
A division of the Countryman Press, Inc.
Woodstock, VT 05091

Text and graphics by Dale Adams
Photographs by Dale Speicher
Text and cover design by Richard Widhu
Printed in the United States of America

Library of Congress Cataloging-in-Publication Data

Adams, Dale.
   25 bicycle tours in eastern Pennsylvania : day trips and
overnights from Philadelphia to the Highlands / Dale Adams and Dale
Speicher. -- 2nd rev. ed.
      p.   cm.
   ISBN 0-88150-127-1 : $8.95
   1. Bicycle touring--Pennsylvania--Guide-books. 2. Pennsylvania-
-Description and travel--1981--Guide-books.   I. Speicher, Dale.
II. Title.   III. Title: Twenty-five bicycle tours in eastern
Pennsylvania.
GV1045.5.P4A3   1989
917.48--dc19   89-31144
                                                          CIP

Acknowledgments

This book would not have been possible without the many people who offered information, made suggestions, or simply allowed us to stay in their homes while we did the research. Many format and content ideas came from *Pennsylvania: A Guide to the Keystone State,* part of the excellent American Guide series of the W.P.A. Writer's Program. Among our many other sources have been various works of Professor Peirce F. Lewis, *Pennsylvania: A Regional Geography* by Raymond E. and Marion Murphy, *Amish Society* by John A. Hostetler, *Outstanding Scenic Geologic Features of Pennsylvania* by Alan R. Geyer and William Bolles, and writings on transportation by William H. Shank. We owe special thanks to Dr. E. Willard Miller, professor emeritus at Penn State University, for his interest, encouragement, and expert information on Pennsylvania.

For the 1989 revised version, we would like to thank the Pennsylvania Department of Transportation, the various county tourist associations, and the many bicyclists who suggested corrections.

Eastern Pennsylvania

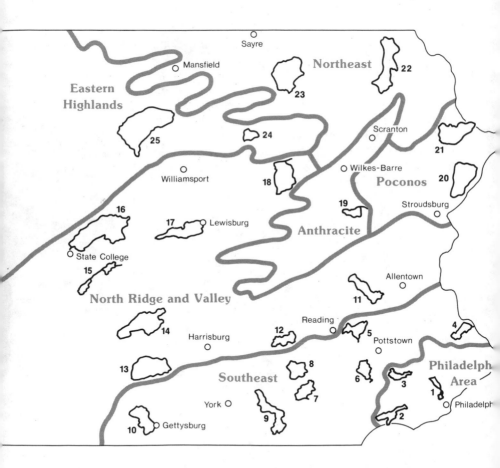

Contents

Introduction

From Independence Hall to the Grand Canyon of Pennsylvania, from fertile Amish farmland to mine-ravaged mountains, from long wooded ridges to lake-dotted plateaus, from market squares to village greens—this is eastern Pennsylvania. The unusual physical and cultural diversity of this area is particularly congenial for bicycling, where moderate speeds, open air, and heightened senses combine to make riders keenly aware of their surroundings. This book helps bicyclists both see Eastern Pennsylvania's diversity and understand it.

Eastern Pennsylvania was the scene of many of this nation's important historical episodes. The Valley Forge encampment, the Battle of Gettysburg, and the United States Centennial are detailed in the writeups of tours which pass through their locations. Less-familiar dramas, such as the settlement of French Royalist refugees on the Susquehanna and life at the Ephrata Cloister, will interest not only bicyclists planning trips in those areas, but all readers who enjoy regional vignettes grand and minor, serious and comical.

Most of all, this is a book of bicycle rides, with maps, directions, and information on things to see, activities to enjoy, and places to stay. Intended for intermediate bicyclists, the tours are designed as much as possible to connect points of interest using little-traveled paved roads, taking the least strenuous routes, passing through interesting and pleasant scenery, and making circular trips of one or two days' length.

Using This Guide

Introductory descriptions to Eastern Pennsylvania's seven regions include information sources, either to supplement what is provided for these tours or for planning additional tours in the region. Most sources are tourist promotion agencies, which unfortunately are better at promoting than they are at providing complete information. Their hotel lists, for example, often include only paying subscribers and miss smaller, interesting inns. Kept in perspective, however, tourist agency information can be useful; lists of events are usually complete and accurate.

Also in these sections are lists of area bicycle clubs for those who wish to join a group—either as a visitor or a member—on a scheduled ride. This approach is strongly suggested for beginning bicycle tourists.

The tour headings give county names for locating the route and for obtaining supplementary maps (see Appendix). Starting places are only suggestions; they have been chosen with accessibility, parking availability, and with the locations of overnight stops in mind. Knowing that one person's hill is another's mountain, terrain descriptions reflect an intermediate bicyclist's perspective. "Flat," "rolling," and "hilly" are the gradations, and a "climb" is a hill of more than one-half mile. Overnight stops are included for possible two-day trips.

Directions are given in the text only for turns or confusing places on the route; otherwise the tour continues straight on the road or numbered highway. Directions are usually in two parts: The first half indicates what to look for, the second half tells what to do. "Intersections" are where the road is crossed by another road;

Rural scene near Elk Hill.

"junctions" are where the road joins another road. State route (SR) signs are white with black letters, about a foot square, and mounted about four feet above the ground; township road (T) signs vary but often look either like legislative route signs or street signs. Directions reading "road to . . . " indicate the presence of a sign pointing the direction to a town or other landmark. An odometer is needed for measuring distances between turns.

Route maps show the locations of major points of interest, lodgings, campgrounds, food stores, and restaurants. Symbols for food stores and restaurants indicate the presence of one or more of those facilities. A "food store" may be anything from a general store to a supermarket. A "restaurant" could be a sandwich shop, a diner, or a fancy establishment.

Safety Tips
☐ Buy a well-fitted bicycle and keep it in good repair
☐ Carry a complete set of tools and know how to use them
☐ Check the mechanical condition of your bicycle before beginning any ride
☐ Do not attempt trips beyond your capabilities
☐ Wear a helmet
☐ Wear bright clothing for visibility; avoid loose-fitting clothes which might get caught in spokes or chain
☐ Ride cautiously and predictably
☐ Signal all turns well in advance and obey other rules of the road
☐ Avoid night riding
☐ Ride double only on lightly-traveled roads, and then be able to quickly form single file when vehicles approach
☐ Walk your bike over metal-floored bridges
☐ Cross railroad tracks at right angles
☐ Watch for sand, loose gravel, wet leaves, and sewer gratings
☐ Test brakes before starting descents
☐ When a dog chases, dismount and walk, keeping your bike between you and the animal. If necessary, use your tire pump in defense
☐ Carry an adequate supply of water

Philadelphia Area

For many, Philadelphia is Independence Hall, the Liberty Bell, and other early American shrines. Some recall street after street of two-story red brick buildings. Others think of the city's native foods: snapper soup, scrapple, and soft pretzels spread with mustard. Still others are reminded of Philadelphia's unique culture, such as the New Year's Day Mummers Parade, when elaborately costumed marchers, jesters, and musicians create a twelve-hour spectacle.

In 1682 William Penn laid out Philadelphia, a grid pattern of streets on a narrow strip of land between the Delaware and Schuylkill Rivers. It would be the chief city of Pennsylvania, the immense tract which King Charles II had given Penn, partly to repay a debt and partly to rid England of this troublesome Quaker. Penn's welcome to persecuted religious groups soon brought to his "City of Brotherly Love" German artisans and English merchants, a combination that launched Philadelphia as a manufacturing center.

The city's central position in the colonies gave it a key role in the country's early history. In 1774 Philadelphia was one of the largest English-speaking cities in the world. The nation's founding fathers came here to hammer out the Declaration of Independence, Articles of Confederation, and the Constitution. Philadelphia was the nation's capital from 1790 to 1800; George Washington served his term as President here. Benjamin Franklin made the city his home, starting in Philadelphia the nation's first library, its first hospital, and its first fire insurance company.

The growth of manufacturing, shipping, and trade in the nineteenth century caused Philadelphia to spread beyond its narrow peninsula. In 1854 it incorporated all other municipalities in Philadelphia County, and the city remains a potpourri of communities, each with its own character, often with an ethnic flavor: Kingessing, North Liberties, Strawberry Mansion, Brewerytown—and 105 more.

The web of railroads around Philadelphia spawned suburban growth, as commuter settlements clustered around stations. "Main Line," a synonym for Philadelphia upper crust, refers to towns along the main line of the Pennsylvania Railroad. The streetcar began filling the interstices, and now the automobile continues suburbanization away from the city into farmland once occupied by country estates and part-time farms of Philadelphia's wealthy.

Philadelphia's historic sites and urban culture make interesting touring, but many of its roads are busy and dangerous. An excellent resource for finding suitable ways through the area is the Bicycle Coalition of the Delaware Valley's *Commuter's Bicycle Map of the Delaware Valley,* which shows the road network in detail, designating reasonably safe roads as well as scenic roads.

For More Information:
Chester County Tourist Promotion Bureau, 117 West Gay Street, West Chester, PA 19380, (800) 228-9933
Delaware County Tourist Bureau, 602 East Baltimore Pike, Media, PA 19063, (215) 565-3679
Philadelphia Convention and Visitors Bureau, 1515 Market Street, Suite 2020, Philadelphia, PA 19102, (800) 321-9563
Valley Forge Area Convention and Visitors Bureau, P.O. Box 311, Norristown, PA 19404, (215) 275-4636

Area Bicycle Clubs:
Bicycle Club of Philadelphia, P.O. Box 30235, Philadelphia, PA 19103
Cycling Enthusiasts of the Delaware Valley, 9325 Marsden Street, Philadelphia, PA 19114
Delaware Valley Bicycle Club, P.O. Box 497, Media, PA 19063
Delaware Valley Council—American Youth Hostels, 35 South Third Street, Philadelphia, PA 19106. Sells the *Guide to Bicycle Touring Routes Between Hostels in Eastern Pennsylvania and New Jersey.*
Pennsylvania Bicycle Club, Box 27535, Philadelphia, PA 19118
Bicycle Coalition of the Delaware Valley, P.O. Box 8194, Philadelphia, PA 19101. Sells the *Commuter's Bicycle Map of the Delaware Valley.*

1 Fairmount Park

- **Philadelphia and Montgomery Counties**
- **Start and end at Philadelphia Museum of Art**
- **27.3 miles; flat with a few hills**
- **1 day**

It was May 10, 1876, the opening day of the United States Centennial in Philadelphia's Fairmount Park. Crowds streamed in under cloudy skies to gather at Memorial Hall, a Beaux-Arts palace. President U.S. Grant arrived with the popular Dom Pedro, Emperor of Brazil. Other dignitaries, including several governors, joined in the speech making. Orchestras and a 1,000-voice choir performed Richard Wagner's "Centennial Grand March," John Greenleaf Whittier's "Centennial Hymn," and Sidney Louier's "Centennial Cantata."

Although world exhibitions were common, pairing one with a celebration of independence was a first. Philadelphia was the obvious site, since it was there that independence was proclaimed and the founding fathers first drafted a constitution. And Philadelphia had expansive Fairmount Park.

Enormous effort and expense went into making the exposition a stupendous event. The largest structure in the park was the Main Exhibition Building, an ornate Victorian edifice of wood, glass, and iron, covering twenty-one acres and holding exhibits of thirty nations. Machinery Hall, covering fourteen acres, held almost every conceivable type of machine. Memorial Hall, a domed granite structure, was built as a permanent art museum. The most striking of all the buildings was Horticultural Hall, a Moorish-style palace of iron, glass, and colored brick. Besides these main buildings, the grounds were filled with smaller structures, headquarters for nations, states, and organizations.

More than eight million people visited the Centennial Exposition during the six months it ran. In addition to its popularity with sightseers, it established the United States internationally as a powerful modern industrial nation.

0.0 (0.0) *From the traffic circle in front of the Philadelphia Museum of Art, follow Kelly Drive.*

The PHILADELPHIA MUSEUM OF ART (10-5 Tues.–Sun.; charge except Sunday before 1), a tan Greco-Roman temple on a knoll above the Schuylkill River, succeeded the Centennial Exposition's Fine Arts Gallery. Opened in 1928, the building is known to many as the place where, in the film *Rocky,* Sylvestor Stallone jumped up and down in the first rays of dawn. To others, the building is an exceptional art museum with 200 galleries holding 100,000 works of art.

FAIRMOUNT PARK is the largest urban park in the United States, with 4,100 acres in the Schuylkill River and Wissahickon Creek Valleys. The park was started in 1812 when the city acquired five acres where the Museum of Art now stands for a municipal waterworks and reservoir. In 1844 the park expanded to protect the water supply from riverside development. The Centennial Exposition was an impetus for further expansion. Much of the land has come from private estates and many eighteenth-century mansions remain, restored to their former appearance and open to the public.

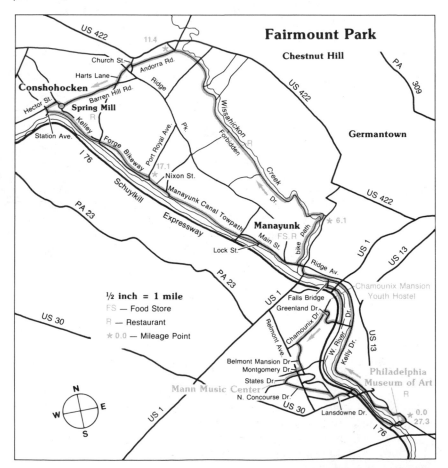

0.4 (0.4) *"Y" at Lincoln Monument; turn left on Kelly Drive. (A bike path parallels the drive to Ridge Avenue. Use this when Kelly Drive is closed to bicyclists during rush hours.)*

On the left is Boat House Row, the 1890s headquarters of Schuylkill rowing clubs. Club members row for recreation or sport. Their shells are designed either for sweeping (when rowers man one oar) or sculling (when rowers use two oars).

The route continues to follow the shore of the placid Schuylkill, with occasional monuments or statues and pleasant picnic areas visited by scavenging Canadian geese.

0.7 Lemon Hill Road, on the right, leads to LEMON HILL (10-4 Wed.–Sun.; charge), the one-time estate of Robert Morris, signer of the Declaration of Independence and financier of the Revolution. Morris lost the estate when his financial empire collapsed and he was sentenced to debtor's prison. The second owner, Henry Pratt, built the present Federal-style mansion in 1800 and turned its surrounding grounds into gardens with lemon trees, giving the estate its name.

1.3 Frederic Remington's sculpture *Cowboy* sits on the right side of the drive facing the river.

2.1 Viewing stand for rowing matches on the left along the river.

3.0 Strawberry Mansion Drive joins on the right.

Follow Strawberry Mansion Drive 0.3 mile to an intersection, then left 0.2 mile to a joining road on left, then 0.1 mile to Woodford. Strawberry Mansion is 0.2 mile beyond Woodford.

WOODFORD (10-5 Tues.-Sun.; charge), built in 1756 with a second story added later, is a Federal brick building with a second-story Palladian window over nine-foot-high entrance doors. Benjamin Franklin was a frequent visitor here.

STRAWBERRY MANSION (10-5 Tues.–Sun.; charge) got its name in the mid-1800s when it was a dairy serving strawberries and cream. The middle of the building is Federal in style, dating to 1790. Matching Greek Revival wings were added in the 1870s. The mansion is furnished in a mixture of Federal, Regency, and Empire styles, reflecting the mansion's varied ownership.

4.4 (4.0) *Where Kelly Drive divides, follow signs onto Ridge Avenue West. (A sidewalk on the left continues to Ridge Avenue. Cyclists may prefer to walk on the sidewalk during heavy traffic periods.)*

This sidewalk is actually part of the Kelly Drive Bikeway and was intended to provide a connection between the wide asphalt path paralleling the drive and the Wissahickon Bikeway. However, it is narrow, on the edge of the highway, under low overhanging trees, and in no way is it safe for bicycling.

4.9 (0.5) *Immediately after crossing Wissahickon Creek, turn right onto an unmarked bike path.*

The bike path follows Wissahickon Creek through a rugged area with exposures of the old Piedmont rock. The Wissahickon Valley was incorporated into Fairmount Park in 1872, and its 1,300 acres have been left in their natural state.

6.1 (1.2) *Junction with Forbidden Drive; turn left.*

FORBIDDEN DRIVE is a packed gravel roadway closed to automobile traffic—therefore "forbidden"—but it is open to strollers, joggers, equestrians, and bicyclists. The sound of traffic eventually fades, tall oaks tower overhead, and the shallow Wissahickon flows alongside.

8.9 Valley Green Inn, a two-story white stucco building, faces the Wissahickon. Late breakfast, lunch, and dinner are served daily (except Christmas) inside the quaintly furnished inn and, in warm weather, outside on a wide porch. A snack bar with benches adjoins the building. This is one of the area's last nineteenth-century wayside inns.

10.3 Within Philadelphia's city limits, a covered bridge spans the Wissahickon on the right.

11.4 (5.3) *End of Forbidden Drive; turn left onto Andorra Road.*

The route travels through an area of modest homes separated by stretches of woods, a surprisingly sparse settlement considering its proximity to Center City. Barns and old farmhouses indicate a formerly agricultural area.

12.3 (0.9) *Junction with Park Avenue; turn right, then immediately left onto Church Street.*

12.5 (0.2) *Intersection with Ridge Pike; go straight onto Harts Lane.*

12.9 (0.4) *Intersection with Barren Hill Road; turn right.*

14.1 Spring Mill, an informal hamlet of stucco, brick, and frame homes, sits in a wooded setting.

14.2 (1.3) *"Y"; bear left onto Hector Street.*

14.4 (0.2) *Intersection; turn left onto Station Avenue.*

14.5 (0.1) *Turn left onto the Valley Forge Bikeway.*

The VALLEY FORGE BIKEWAY is a twenty-five mile conglomeration of towpaths, railroad grades, and sidewalks for hiking and bicycling. The Spring Mill section, paved and flat, follows an abandoned railroad grade through an area abounding in wildflowers and weeds.

17.1 (2.6) *Junction with Port Royal Avenue (unmarked); turn right, then immediately left onto Nixon Street.*

17.4 (0.3) *Where the main road turns left, go straight; then immediately turn right across railroad tracks.*

17.5 (0.1) *Junction with Manayunk Canal Towpath; turn left.*

The MANAYUNK CANAL TOWPATH, another part of the Philadelphia-Valley Forge trail, is a packed gravel path which follows the Manayunk Canal, a section of the Schuylkill Canal system built in 1819. From the towpath there are views of the Schuylkill River and occasionally of old brick and concrete industrial structures. Later, the bikeway skirts the town of Manayunk, at times using boardwalks along the canal. The canal is a local water supply and a popular fishing hole for Manayunkers, although it appears to yield as many old boots as fish.

19.7 (2.2) *End of towpath at Lock Street; turn left, then immediately right onto Main Street in Manayunk.*

MANAYUNK, once known as the Manchester of America, is an old industrial town built on a steep hillside. As the slope increases, a number of streets become stairs. Although the town is now incorporated into Philadelphia, it remains a distinct community with residential and business sections. Many of the homes and businesses are decrepit, but Manayunk is beginning to attract young Philadelphians, who are opening organic food stores, selling antiques, and rehabilitating row houses.

20.5 (0.8) *Junction with Ridge Avenue; turn right and follow signs onto Kelly Drive.*

21.4 (0.9) *Turn right over Falls Bridge, then turn left onto West River Drive. (A bike path parallels West River Drive. Use this when West River Drive is closed to bicyclists during rush hours.)*

There was once a waterfall here, but it was obliterated by the building of a dam. This is the "fall line," a zone that extends along the East Coast where the old crystalline rock of the Piedmont to the west joins the loose, unconsolidated sand and clay of the Coastal Plain to the east. Piedmont rocks are resistant to stream erosion, so streams descending to the sea through them form narrow gorges with waterfalls and rapids. But when the streams contact the weak material of the Coastal Plain, they widen and slow.

Since the falls were a source of industrial power, a number of American cities, including Georgetown, Baltimore, and Richmond, were established on the fall line. The fall line is also the upper limit of navigation from the sea, a good location for commercial centers.

During rush hours West River Drive becomes one way, to accommodate morning in-bound and afternoon out-bound traffic.

22.3 (0.9) *Turn right onto the ramp to Greenland Drive, then right onto Greenland Drive.*

The route continues through the manicured grounds of Fairmount Park.

23.0 (0.7) *"Y"; bear left onto Chamounix Drive.*

Right on Chamounix Drive to its end, 0.3 mile, is CHAMOUNIX MANSION (215-878-3676) an American Youth Hostel. The two and a half-story structure was built in 1800 by a Quaker merchant. The mansion offers typical hostel dorms, a kitchen, and a common room. Nonmembers can buy an introductory pass. Check-in time is 4:30-8:00.

23.2 (0.2) *Turn left onto Belmont Mansion Drive.*

23.4 The front of Belmont Mansion offers a stunning view of Philadelphia's skyline over the plush greenery of Fairmount Park, its many skyscrapers surrounding the Second Empire tower of City Hall.

23.8 (0.6) *Intersection with Montgomery Drive; turn right (west). (Montgomery Drive is one-way eastbound weekdays 7-10 a.m.)*

Straight ahead 0.4 mile is the HORTICULTURE CENTER (9-3 Wed.-Sun.; free) consisting of a greenhouse, gardens, and an arboretum holding some specimens from the Centennial's Horticulture

Frederic Remington statue of a cowboy, one of the many sculptures found throughout Fairmount Park.

Hall. Here also is the JAPANESE HOUSE (Apr.–Oct., 10-4 Wed.–Sun.; charge), an authentic reconstruction of a seventeenth-century Japanese scholar's house, tea house, and garden.

24.0 (0.2) *Intersection with Belmont Avenue; turn left, then immediately right onto States Drive.*

At this junction is Ohio House, a Victorian Gothic cottage, the only state building remaining from the Centennial Exposition.

24.03 (0.3) *Catholic Total Abstinence Fountain; follow the traffic circle, pass the first spoke, then turn right onto the second spoke, North Concourse Drive.*

The CATHOLIC TOTAL ABSTINENCE FOUNTAIN, remaining from the Centennial, has statues of four great Revolutionary War Catholics (teetotalers, no doubt) surrounding Moses on a pedestal. Originally a drinking fountain, it was built as an alternative to Philadelphia's numerous saloons.

25.0 Domed MEMORIAL HALL, the last of the Exhibition's major buildings, is on the left. Formerly an art gallery, it now holds park offices and recreational facilities, including an indoor swimming pool. An outdoor pool is adjacent to the structure.

25.2 The two columns of the SMITH MEMORIAL flank the roadway. Quarter-circle stone benches extend from the monument on each side of the road. These are the mysterious WHISPERING BENCHES. Two people sitting at the far ends of one of these benches can still converse in whispers.

25.4 (1.1) *Junction with Lansdowne Drive; turn left.*

25.7 (0.3) *Turn left under Schuylkill Expressway, then immediately right on West River Drive. (A bike path parallels the drive.)*

Straight here 0.2 mile is the PHILADELPHIA ZOOLOGICAL GARDEN (9:30-5 weekdays, 9:30-6 weekends; charge), America's first zoo. Covering 42 acres, it houses 1,700 animals.

On the left, views appear of the Schuylkill River, the river dam, Boat House Row, the Greek Revival pavillions of the Water Works on the opposite shore, and the Museum of Art above them on a hill.

27.3 (1.6) *Philadelphia Museum of Art.*

Bicycle Shops:
Philadelphia Discount Bicycle Center, 826 North Broad, Philadelphia, (215) 765-9118
Roxy Bicycle Shop, 4264 Manayunk Avenue, Philadelphia, (215) 487-2050
Wolff Cycle, 4311 Lancaster Avenue, Philadelphia, (215) 222-2171
Bicycle Technology, 13th and Locust Streets, Philadelphia, (215) 735-1503
Saile J. & Sons, 4325 Main (Manayunk), Philadelphia, (215) 483-3535
Gerace Bicycle Shop, 1013 Reed Street, Philadelphia, (215) 468-2558
L. Ponnock, 1028 Arch Street, Philadelphia, (215) 923-1310

2 Brandywine Creek

- **Chester and Delaware Counties**
- **Start and end at Tyler Arboretum**
- **40.4 miles; rolling with some hills**
- **1 day**

In late August of 1777, during the third year of the War for Independence, British General William Howe landed in Maryland with 15,000 troops. He intended to capture Philadelphia, the capitol of the rebelling colonies. On September 11, these forces reached Brandywine Creek, where General George Washington had laid a defense line along the east bank.

General Howe feinted a main frontal attack with 5,000 troops at Chadds Ford, but he directed the bulk of his forces north to strike Washington's right flank from the rear. When Washington realized this, he moved his right flank to a hill at Birmingham Meetinghouse in line with Howe's movements.

Late in the afternoon, the Continental Army was forced to draw back and reposition at Dilworthtown. For a while the British advance was held, but munitions ran low and the Americans had to retreat. The situation was no better at the Brandywine, where the outnumbered Continentals retreated to Chester. Despite a noble effort, the Americans had lost, and the British were on their way to Philadelphia.

0.0 (0.0) *Leaving the Tyler Arboretum parking area, turn right onto Painter Road.*

The TYLER ABORETUM (9–4 weekdays; 10–4 weekends; charge), a single tract of 700 acres with woods, fields, gardens, and horticultural collections, was the estate of Thomas Minshall, who received the land from William Penn in 1681. The land belonged to Minshall's descendants until 1945, when it was bequeathed as an arboretum for public use. Among the many interesting sights in the park is a giant sequoia—a large tree by Pennsylvania standards, but one that needs hundreds of years to compete with its Western cousins.

0.5 (0.5) *Intersection with PA 352; go straight onto Forge Road.*

1.7 (1.2) *Immediately after passing a joining road on the left, turn right onto Valley Road (SR 4005).*

2.3 (0.6) *Left onto Sweet Water Road (SR 4016).*

Typical of this tour, the route here passes through rolling

countryside with a mixture of farms and woodlots. Except for occasional places into which Philadelphia suburbia has advanced, the area is sparsely populated.

3.5 (1.2) *Stop sign; turn left over a bridge into Glen Mills, then go straight onto Glen Mills Road.*
   4.1 The complex of red brick buildings on the right is the Glen

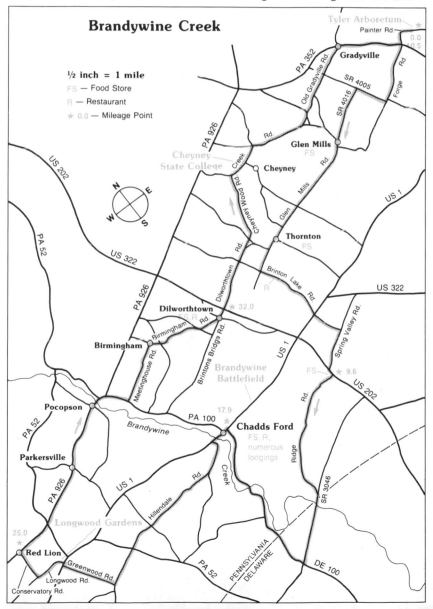

Mills School, an institution for wayward boys.

5.9 The village of Thornton's main enterprises, its post office and a small grocery store, are located in one two-story building with a long first-floor porch.

6.1 (2.6) *"Y"; bear left on Glen Mills Road.*

6.6 (0.5) *Intersection with Brinton Lake Road; turn left.*

8.7 (2.1) *Junction with Spring Valley Road; turn right.*
The route passes through slightly rolling farmland with pastures, cornfields, small woods, and occasional subdivisions.

9.6 (0.9) *Junction with US 202; turn left, then after 0.1 mile turn right onto Ridge Road. (Use care on busy US 202.)*

10.6 On the left is a white stucco octagonal house, a style popular during the Victorian period. Orson Fowler, American inventor of the octagonal house, touted the beauty of its form, its economy of materials, its functional interior, and the possibility of eight views.

12.5 (2.9) *Junction with SR 3046; turn right.*

14.1 (1.6) *Intersection with DE 100; turn right.*
Delaware Route 100, which becomes PA 100, follows the valley of BRANDYWINE CREEK, a stream with a length of about sixty miles. Legends say the creek got its name from its faintly golden color, like *brandewign* or Dutch gin, or from a liquor-laden ship sunk by ice in the river's estuary. More likely the word came from "Brantwyn," the surname of a Swede who settled in the lower valley.

The Brandywine flows through low, partially wooded hills. The area is known for its large stone homes and horse pastures edged with white post-and-rail fences.

17.9 (3.8) *Junction with US 1 in Chadds Ford; turn left.*
Right 0.7 mile from this junction is the BRANDYWINE BATTLE-FIELD PARK (9-5 Tues.–Sat., 12-5 Sun., closed certain holidays; charge for historic buildings) which holds the reconstructed headquarters of George Washington and the restored quarters of General Lafayette. A visitors center offers exhibits and a slide presentation. There are picnic areas on the battlefield.

CHADDS FORD is a village of antique shops, gift shops, and museums spread along a busy highway. During the early 1700s the site was an important post on a major road leading west. John Chadd started a ferry and an inn here in 1737, and in 1777 Washington's troops were positioned here to defend Philadelphia.

The area is also known for artists who have contributed to a tradition in American art known as the "Brandywine Heritage." The first of these artists was Howard Pyle, the famous illustrator, who began teaching here in the summer of 1898. Chadds Ford has also been the home of three Wyeth family generations.

In 1971 the Brandywine Conservancy, a group dedicated to preserving the environmental quality and cultural heritage of the region, opened the BRANDYWINE RIVER MUSEUM (9:30-4:30 daily except Christmas, 215-338-7601; charge). The museum, a Civil War grist mill with a modern addition overlooking the Brandywine, holds work of the Wyeths as well as that of other Brandywine and American artists. The museum is located on US 1 in Chadds Ford and has special events and changing exhibits.

18.4 (0.5) *After crossing Brandywine River, turn left onto Hillendale Road (unmarked).*

19.3 (0.9) *"Y"; bear right over the railroad tracks on Hillendale Road (unmarked).*

21.5 (2.2) *Intersection with PA 52; go straight on Hillendale Road.*

22.3 (0.8) *Turn right onto Greenwood Road (unmarked).*

The route passes through a mostly wooded area with sparse residential development.

23.4 (1.1) *Junction with US 1; turn right, then after 0.1 mile take a ramp onto an overpass.*

23.8 (0.4) *Immediately after the overpass, turn left onto Longwood Road (unmarked).*

Straight ahead is LONGWOOD GARDENS (9–6 daily, 215-388-6741; charge), the former estate of Pierre S. duPont. The land was originally conveyed to George Pierce by William Penn in 1701. Pierce built a brick house here in 1730; it is now part of the duPont residence. The estate got its name before the Civil War when runaway slaves gave this stop on the Underground Railroad the name "Long Woods."

Longwood Gardens includes 350 acres of outdoor gardens and woodlands, glass conservatories covering twenty indoor gardens, fountains, and the duPont House. On Tuesday and Saturday evenings during the summer there is an illuminated fountain display. Evening performances of music, much of it classical, are given throughout the year.

24.3 (0.5) *Turn right onto Conservatory Road.*

The route passes through manicured roadsides along the gardens.

25.0 (0.7) *Junction with PA 926 in Red Lion; turn right.*

28.4 (3.4) *Junction with PA 100; turn right.*

29.0 (0.6) *Turn left onto Meetinghouse Road.*
Here on a narrow lane begins a gradual climb from the Brandywine Valley past horse pastures and old farmsteads, the estates of the rural gentry. There are views of rolling woodlands and fields along the Brandywine.

30.3 (1.3) *Junction with Birmingham Road; turn right.*
Here is BIRMINGHAM MEETING, the 1763 Quaker meeting-house that witnessed the major part of the Battle of Brandywine. In a shaded graveyard next to the building lie the bodies of unknown soldiers killed in that battle. Nearby are several monuments commemorating the battle, including memorials to Lafayette and Pulaski.

30.7 By a house on the left is a small monument marking the site where General Lafayette was wounded during the Battle of Brandywine.

31.8 (1.5) *Junction in Dilworthtown; turn right, then immediately left onto Brintons Bridge Road.*
DILWORTHTOWN was the place where Americans, retreating from the Birmingham Meeting battle, repositioned and fought until their ammunition ran out. The village today is a Historic District on the National Register. There are good examples of the stone and

stuccoed-stone Quaker architecture common in this area. The two-story brick Dilworth House, built in 1758 and long operated as an inn, is now part of the Dilworthtown Inn, a restaurant. A gift shop occupies a former general store. Across the street a blacksmith makes hinges, door handles, and other ornamental pieces.

> South of Dilworthtown 0.5 mile on the West Chester-Wilmington Pike is the BRINTON 1704 HOUSE, (May–Oct., 1–4 Tues., Thurs., and Sat. except holidays; charge), a Quaker farmhouse which has been returned to its original appearance and opened to the public. The two-story stone house, an example of medieval English architecture, was built by William Brinton, a second generation Quaker. His descendants have meticulously restored the building and furnished it with period pieces. Visitors are taken through the house by a knowledgeable guide, sometimes a family member.

32.0 (0.2) *Intersection with US 322-202; go straight onto Dilworthtown Road.*

33.4 (1.4) *"Y", bear left onto Cheyney Woods Road.*

34.8 (1.4) *Junction; turn right onto Creek Road (unmarked).*

The route passes CHEYNEY STATE COLLEGE, on the left. Formerly a trade school for blacks, it is now a state-supported liberal arts college, and it still has a large black population.

35.7 (0.9) *Intersection; turn right on Creek Road.*

36.9 (1.2) *Turn left onto Old Gradyville Road.*

37.1 (0.2) *"Y"; bear right on Old Gradyville Road.*

38.6 (1.5) *Intersection with PA 352; turn right.*

> Straight ahead here the road leads to RIDLEY CREEK STATE PARK. A major attraction in the park is the COLONIAL PENNSYLVANIA PLANTATION (Apr.–Nov., 10-5 weekends, 215-566-1725; charge), a Delaware County Quaker farm maintained as it was in 1776. It is a living museum with demonstrations of farm crafts. Special events through the year include military reenactments and colonial feasts.

39.3 (1.3) *Intersection with Forge Road; turn left.*

40.4 (0.5) *Tyler Arboretum.*

Bicycle Shops:
None on route. The nearest shops are in West Chester, Downington, and Media.

3 Valley Forge

- **Chester and Montgomery Counties**
- **Start and end at Valley Forge National Historic Park**
- **27.9 miles; rolling with some hills**
- **1 day**

The Battle of Brandywine was lost, and no gains had been made at Germantown. Washington's army was battle worn, poorly clothed, and down in spirits. The winter of 1777 was coming on, so a place was needed to recover, retrain, and wait for the following spring. Washington chose Valley Forge because it was close enough to the British in Philadelphia to protect the southeastern Pennsylvania countryside, yet far enough away to be safe from surprise enemy attacks. Soldiers were practically naked, many without shoes, and sick from a variety of diseases. Because of incompetence in the quartermaster and commissary departments, flour and water were sometimes the only available nourishment. Similar problems existed in the medical corps, preventing adequate care of the sick and wounded. Nearly 3,000 men died from diseases or freezing.

But as the cold winter days slowly passed, this army experienced a remarkable transformation. It was due in part to Washington's leadership and the arrival of his spouse "Lady Washington," who joined other women in nursing the sick and making clothes for protection against the cold. Baron Friedrich Wilhelm von Steuben, an experienced Prussian drillmaster, came from Europe at the behest of Benjamin Franklin. Von Steuben tirelessly worked the poorly trained men until they were efficient soldiers. Major General Nathanael Greene, Washington's right-hand man, was charged with the quartermaster department, and soon he had rounded up the needed food and supplies.

When spring arrived, new recruits began filling the thinned ranks. Morale rose when news came that France had joined America in the war. Word came, too, that the British were leaving Philadelphia for New York. On June 19, the Continental Army, disciplined, better equipped, and with renewed spirit, left to pursue the enemy in New Jersey.

0.0 (0.0) *Leaving the entrance to the Valley Forge National Historic Park visitors center, turn left onto Outer Line Drive.*

VALLEY FORGE HISTORIC PARK, the place where the ragged Continentals camped, is an extensive park with drives and bike paths which connect remains and reconstructions of major forts

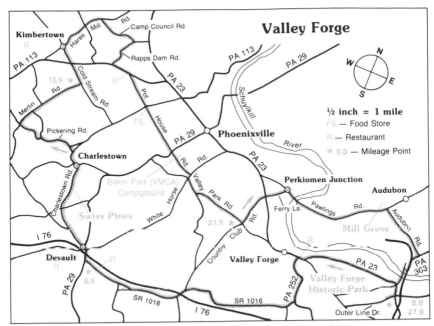

and lines of earthworks, reconstructed huts, memorials, and the renovated quarters of officers, including Washington's head-quarters.

The VISITORS CENTER (8:30–6 daily; free), a modern glass building partially underground, houses exhibits of the Valley Forge encampment and offers audio-visual presentations recounting the ordeal. A concessionaire rents one- and three-speed bicycles on weekends in the spring and fall, and through the week during June, July, and August.

0.1 (0.1) *Intersection; turn left onto PA 23. (A bike path parallels PA 23 as far as Washington's Headquarters.)*

1.2 On the right is the WASHINGTON MEMORIAL CHAPEL, a stone Gothic structure. The chapel, which holds regular services through the week, contains hand-carved stone and wood work, stained glass windows, and flags, all representing some aspect of the nation's history or honoring a particular person or group. George Washington is the prominent honoree.

The tower attached to the chapel is the WASHINGTON MEM-ORIAL NATIONAL CARILLON and BELL MUSEUM (10–4 daily). Visitors can climb a narrow winding stone staircase to an enclosed platform near the top of the tower, where a carillonneur will explain the instrument, which has a keyboard arranged like a piano but which is played with the fists. This carillon has fifty-eight bells. Fifty-seven represent the states and territories, and one is the National Birthday Bell.

In the crypt of the Bell Tower is the Bell Museum containing over 800 bells, some dating before the birth of Christ. Also at the chapel is the VALLEY FORGE HISTORICAL SOCIETY MUSEUM (9:30–4 Mon.–Sat., 1–4 Sunday; charge), holding artifacts of the Revolution.

1.6 The two-story stone farmhouse on the left served as the quarters of General James Varnum. The building has been restored to look as it did during Varnum's occupancy, and an interpreter in period dress is stationed at the site. The building overlooks the Grand Parade, the field where Von Steuben drilled Continental troops.

2.6 WASHINGTON'S HEADQUARTERS (8:30-6 daily; charge) is another stone house, which Washington sublet from Widow Deborah Hewes. Washington originally promised his suffering troops that he would tent and not seek better shelter until they, too, could move indoors. But on Christmas Day a heavy snowfall forced Washington into this building.

2.8 (2.7) *Left onto PA 252.*

The highway follows Valley Creek through a wooded area. This stream separates MOUNT JOY on the left and MOUNT MISERY on the right. Two explorers, one of whom is said to have been William Penn, are supposed to have become lost after wandering from their camp on the Schuylkill. They spent a miserable night on a hill which they named Mount Misery. Towards dawn they crossed a stream and climbed another hill, from which they saw their camp—this hill they named Mount Joy.

3.8 (1.0) *Turn right over a covered bridge onto SR 1016.*

The route passes wealthy estates with horse pastures, and the modern Colonials of Philadelphia commuters. The land is gently rolling, a mixture of woods and fields.

8.6 (4.8) *Junction with PA 29; turn right.*

8.8 (0.2) *Intersection; go straight onto Charlestown Road.*

9.3 (0.5) *"Y"; bear right on Charlestown Road.*

10.5 On the right is SWISS PINES PARK (10–4 Mon.–Fri., 9–noon Sat; free), which includes a formal Japanese garden and springtime rhododendron displays. Trails weave through the garden past a small carp pond, a sand garden, and numerous sculptures.

10.8 Charlestown is a hamlet of stone buildings. The early settlers who built these structures used building techniques they had learned in England, where wood was a scarce material. Later builders finally realized they were in one of the world's largest forests and abandoned stone and half-timbered architecture.

11.0 (1.7) *Turn left onto Pickering Road.*

11.9 (0.9) *"Y"; bear left over the bridge on Pickering Road.*

12.4 (0.5) *Intersection with Merlin Road; turn right.*
At this intersection are several old stone houses of the Georgian style. One has been plastered and whitewashed, a common exterior for old buildings around Philadelphia. Stucco is thought to be an English contribution to the Pennsylvania landscape. Besides improving appearance, plaster and whitewash have several practical advantages. Plaster insulates in the winter and its white color reflects heat during the summer. Stucco also protects stone, brick, or half-timbered walls from the weather.

13.9 (1.5) *Junction with Cold Stream Road; turn left.*

14.8 (0.9) *Intersection in Kimberton; turn right onto Hares Mill Road.*
KIMBERTON, a crossroads settlement, has many stone and stuccoed buildings, giving it the air of an English village. It was founded in 1817, when a Quaker schoolmaster organized a boarding school for girls here. This quaint community has several antique shops. The post office is in an old stone mill.

   15.5 Intersection with Seven Stars Road.
   Left here 0.3 mile is the KENNEDY COVERED BRIDGE. There is swimming in the stream beneath the bridge.

15.9 (1.1) *After crossing a bridge, turn right onto Camp Council Road.*

16.7 (0.8) *Junction with Rapps Dam Road; turn right over Rapps Covered Bridge.*
RAPPS COVERED BRIDGE is a one-span, Burr truss bridge. The Burr truss, the most common of several covered bridge designs, is identified by a curved beam on the interior of each side.

17.4 (0.7) *Junction with PA 113; turn left.*

17.8 (0.4) *Turn right onto Pot House Road (unmarked).*

   19.7 The YMCA Baker Park (May–Oct., 215-933-5865) has a camping area with showers which is open to both members and nonmembers. A swimming pool is open to members and campers only.

      Proximity to the King of Prussia interchange, with easy access to Philadelphia, has put residential developments and apartment complexes next to farm fields on this road.

20.3 (2.5) *Junction with White Horse Road; turn right, then after crossing Pickering Creek turn left onto Valley Park Road.*

White fences surrounding horse pastures and large old farmhouses which belong to gentlemen farmers border the roadway.

21.9 (1.6) *Intersection with Country Club Road; turn left.*

22.7 (0.8) *Intersection with PA 23; go straight onto Ferry Lane.*

23.2 (0.5) *Junction with Pawlings Road in Perkiomen Junction; turn right.*

25.0 Fatland, the white mansion on the knoll at the right, was the estate of William Bakewell, whose daughter married John James Audubon.

25.4 (2.2) *Turn right onto Audubon Road.*

At this junction is the entrance to MILL GROVE (10-4 Tues.– Sat., 1-4 Sun.; free), the home from 1804 to 1806 of John James

Washington's Headquarters, Valley Forge National Historic Park.

Audubon, the famous ornithologist and painter. The building, which dates to 1762, is two-and-a-half stories tall, made of stone, and it sits on a slope above Perkiomen Creek. Here Audubon studied local wildlife, began nature painting, and made his home into a veritable natural history museum.

After marrying Lucy Bakewell, Audubon left Mill Grove and began a life of roaming the countryside in search of creatures to hunt, trap, and sketch. His business failures, the sufferings of his wife and children, and his odd preoccupations earned him the reputation of a shiftless fellow. But all this changed in 1838 when he completed his folio edition of *Birds of America*, a work which sold by subscription at $1,000 a set.

26.2 (1.2) *Junction with PA 363; turn right. (Caution: heavy traffic.)*

26.4 (0.2) *Where PA 363 continues right to US 422, bear left and follow road to the Old Betzwood Bridge.*

27.2 The BETZWOOD PICNIC AREA is on the right along the Schuylkill River.

27.5 (0.4) *Junction with PA 23; turn left.*

27.8 (0.3) *Intersection; turn right onto Outer Line Drive, then go 0.1 mile to the Valley Forge visitors center.*

Bicycle Shops:
Phoenixville Bike Line, 711 Nutt Road, Phoenixville, (215) 935-9111

Southeast

The southeastern corner of Pennsylvania is like a gently sloping garden with a rock wall along its northwestern border. The rock layers here were extremely distorted by the building of the Appalachians, but most have been worn down by erosion to a rich, gently rolling farmland, the Piedmont. Two segments of the Blue Ridge, made of tougher rock, form a rugged forest-covered barrier, the garden's rock wall.

The amazingly fertile land—some of the best in the country—drew German settlers starting in the early 1700s. Leaving war-torn and intolerant Europe, they accepted William Penn's offer of prosperity and religious freedom in Pennsylvania. Commonly referred to as the Pennsylvania Dutch (after an early mistranslation of "Deutsch"), they have given this area its own culture, including distinctive architecture, art, dress, dialect, and food. The Dunkards, Amish, and Mennonites—the plain sects—retain most aspects of the culture, but even less traditional Pennsylvania Germans—a sizeable number of Pennsylvanians—still speak the dialect, enjoy the cuisine, or practice the German religions of their forefathers. A major celebration of the Pennsylvania Dutch culture is the Kutztown Folk Festival, held the first week of July.

The Southeast is crisscrossed by a myriad of paved back roads and country lanes, which are more enjoyable for bicycling than the busy state and federal highways. The terrain is generally not strenuous, since it is hilly in a few areas (such as the segments of the Blue Ridge), but practically flat in the limestone lowlands near Lancaster and York, and only slightly rolling elsewhere. A well-populated tourist area, the Southeast has many lodgings, food-stores, and other facilities.

For More Information:

Berks County Visitors Information Association, Sheraton Berkshire Inn, Route 422 West, Paper Mill Road Exit, Wyomissing, PA 19610, (215) 375-4085

Bucks County Tourist Commission, 152 Swamp Road, Doylestown, PA 18901, (215) 345-4552

Chester County Tourist Promotion Bureau, 117 West Gay Street, West Chester, PA 19380, (800) 228-9933

Gettysburg Travel Council, 35 Carlisle Street, Gettysburg, PA 17325, (717) 334-6274

Lancaster Mennonite Conference Historical Society, 2215 Mill Stream Road, Lancaster, PA 17602, (717) 393-9745

Pennsylvania Dutch Convention and Visitors Bureau, 501 Greenfield Road, Lancaster, PA 17601, (717) 299-8901

York County Convention and Visitors Bureau, 1 Marketway East, P.O. Box 1229, York, PA 17405, (717) 848-4000

Area Bicycle Clubs:

Berks County Bicycle Club, P.O. Box 8264, Reading, PA 19603

Brandywine Bicycle Club, 1221 Hayesville-Lincoln Road, Oxford, PA 19363

Central Bucks Bicycle Club, P.O. Box 295, Buckingham, PA 18912

Delaware Valley Council—American Youth Hostels, 35 South Third Street, Philadelphia, PA 19106. Sells a guide with tours between hostels in Eastern Pennsylvania and New Jersey.

Gettysburg Bicycle Club, 303 S. Washington Street, Gettysburg, PA 17325

Harrisburg Bicycle Club, 16 East Green Street, Shiremanstown, PA 17011

Hanover Cyclers, 129 Baltimore Street, Hanover, PA 17331

Lancaster Bicycle Club, P.O. Box 535, Lancaster, PA 17603. Publishes a guidebook series of 26 rides, mostly within Lancaster County.

Tri-County Pedalers, 323 High Street, Pottstown, PA 19464

York Bicycle Club, P.O. Box 1541, York, PA 17405

The towpath along the Delaware Canal.

4 New Hope

- **Bucks County**
- **Start and end at Doylestown**
- **26.7 miles; flat to rolling with a few climbs**
- **1 day**

Passenger boats, or packets, traveled on Pennsylvania's extensive canal system of the 1800s. Long and low to pass beneath bridges, each contained rooms for ladies, gentlemen, cooking, and cargo. The gentlemen's room was the daytime gathering place for everyone on board. It had a bar and tables for meals, in addition to the men's bunks stacked against the walls. The ladies' room, separated from the men's room by a red curtain, was finer in its decoration. It also had bunks and tables.

The cramped packet was far from luxury transportation. A replacement team of horses housed in the front of the boat added its own odors to those of the bar, the kitchen, and the passengers. The common room was filled with snoring old men, gossiping women, and crying children. More spacious accommodations on deck required ducking at each call of "low bridge."

At night three-tier bunks suspended by cords were set up. Charles Dickens, who traveled through Pennsylvania by canal, first mistook these for bookshelves, but then he realized that "the passengers were the library and that they were to be arranged edgewise on the shelves till morning." Frequently the packet's grating against a lock or against another boat at night would send some members flying and arouse the entire party.

Dickens also recalled some enjoyable aspects of canal travel, such as the exhilaration of washing in the morning with cold canal water. "The fast, brisk walk upon the towing-path between that time and breakfast, when every vein and artery seemed to tingle with health; the exquisite beauty of the opening day, when light came gleaming off from everything; the lazy motion of the boat, when one lay idly on the deck, looking through rather than at the deep blue sky, the gliding on at night, so noiselessly, the shining out of the bright stars, undisturbed by noise of wheels or steam or any other sound than the liquid rippling of the water as the boat went on; all these were pure delights."

0.0 (0.0) *Leaving the parking area for Mercer Museum in Doylestown, turn left onto Scout Way, then after 0.1 mile turn left onto Pine Street.*

The MERCER MUSEUM (10-5:00 Mon.–Sat., 1-5 Sun.;

charge), is a tall concrete structure with various wings, an assortment of windows, and altogether a castle-like appearance. Henry
Mercer, an archaeologist and anthropologist, designed this unusual building in the early twentieth century to house his collection
of early American tools. Inside, a lofty well reaches from the ground
floor to the roof. On surrounding balconies, farm implements, Colonial furniture, cider presses, and other relics are displayed. Heavy
agricultural implements, Conestoga wagons, and other cumber-
some objects extend out into the well, suspended by wires and
chains.

0.4 (0.4) *Junction with Court Street; turn right.*
      An early stage stop for travelers between Easton and Phila-
delphia, DOYLESTOWN dates back to a settlement of the Doyle
family around 1730. One of the structures surviving from the
Colonial period is the Fountain House at the northwestern corner of

State and Main Streets. Built in 1758 and the oldest of the remaining taverns, it is a stuccoed building, three and a half stories tall, with a mansard roof which was added later. Doylestown's chief growth came, however, in the mid-1800s when it was a county seat and railroad stop. That period's Victorian charm is still present today.

Following Court Street, the route passes through a neighborhood of early twentieth century homes. One common style is the California Bungalow, with one story, an attic, and a roof that makes a porch on the front. This was California's first major contribution to the common architecture of America.

1.1 On the left is FONTHILL (215-348-9461), the chateau-like former estate of Dr. Mercer. Built between 1890 and 1910, the buildings are mostly made of reinforced concrete with red tile roofs and variously shaped windows, dormers, and chimneys. The interiors are richly decorated with tile and filled with treasures from Mercer's explorations throughout the world.

Near Fonthill is Mercer's MORAVIAN POTTERY AND TILE WORKS (10-5 daily; charge), a U-shaped structure also made of reinforced concrete, with Spanish mission features. Here Mercer produced tiles inspired by the designs of Moravian craftsmen. Now a living history museum, the tile works offers demonstrations of tile making.

1.3 (0.9) *Junction with PA 313; turn right, then immediately left onto North Chubb Drive.*

The next ring in the outward growth of Doylestown is this neighborhood dating to the 1940s and 1950s, which includes styles such as the Cape Cod Cottage. Porches have started to disappear with the coming of T.V. and air conditioning. Lawns, an American status symbol, are getting larger.

1.8 (0.5) *Turn left onto Glen Road.*

This neighborhood consists of ranchers and split-levels of the 1950s and 1960s. Lawns are even larger.

2.1 (0.3) *Where Glen Road ends, bear right onto Buttonwood Drive.*

2.5 (0.4) *Junction with Smoke Road; turn left.*

2.8 (0.3) *Junction with Church School Road (unmarked); turn right.*

The landscape here is nearly flat, with fields bordered by hedgerows.

3.2 (0.4) *Intersection with Mechanicsville Road; turn left.*
Modern homes mixed with old stone farmsteads are surrounded by cornfields.

7.6 (4.4) *Intersection with Aquetong Road; go straight onto Mechanicsville Road.*

9.9 (2.3) *Intersection with PA 263 in Solebury; go straight, then at a "Y" bear right onto T 402.*
   11.2 The Solebury Friends Meeting is a white-shuttered stone building with two front doors. It stands in a grove of maples. Across the road is a graveyard with typically small Quaker tombstones.

12.0 (2.1) *Turn left onto Sugan Road.*

12.8 (0.8) *"Y"; bear left over tracks onto West Mechanic Street.*

13.4 (0.6) *Turn left onto Stocton Avenue.*

13.5 (0.1) *Junction with Ferry Street in New Hope; reverse direction on Stocton Avenue, then turn right onto Mechanic Street.*
   A ferry landing settled in the early 1700s, NEW HOPE was once known as Coryell's Ferry, but the town renamed itself after the New Hope Mills. These mills replaced mills destroyed by fire, giving new hope to the community.
   In 1832 New Hope became a port on the DELAWARE CANAL, which extended from Easton to navigable water of the Delaware River at Bristol. The canal's principal traffic was coal transferred from the Lehigh Canal at Easton and bound for Philadelphia. The canal operated until 1931. Soon after its closing, the canal became the linear Roosevelt State Park. To this day it is maintained close to its old operating condition. The towpath is a popular walking path.
   At the turn of the century, New Hope's canal, rustic homes, and old mills attracted painters and writers who formed an artists' colony. Like many other artists' colonies, New Hope has become a tourist mecca with craft shops and ice cream parlors, and crowded streets on summer weekends. The town is also a well-known gay resort.
   A partial escape from the town's commercialism is found along the canal, which flows by backyards and behind buildings. At several points a cafe overlooks the canal and sometimes a stairway leads to a basement craft shop. Open mule-drawn passenger barges carry tourists, often accompanied by musicians, along the

canal. For information on hours and rates phone the New Hope Barge Company at (215) 862-2842.

The Lower Delaware River is known for its quaint inns. A popular activity is walking from one to another along the canal towpath. The Logan Inn (215-862-2300), built in New Hope in 1727, is supposed to have been host to George Washington five times. The inn is furnished with antiques; it serves lunch and dinner, and it offers rooms with or without baths.

14.0 (0.5) *"Y"; bear left onto Stoney Hill Road.*

14.3 (0.3) *Junction; turn left, then immediately right on Stoney Hill Road.*

The route makes a gradual climb from the Delaware River past stuccoed homes in a generally wooded area.

17.2 (2.9) *Intersection with Street Road; turn right.*

18.4 (1.2) *Intersection with Upper Mountain Road; turn left.*

Because this area was settled by English Quakers, its farmsteads lack the large barns seen in the German-settled lowlands.

19.6 (1.2) *Junction with Holicong Road; turn left, then immediately right onto Upper Mountain Road.*

20.9 (1.3) *Junction with PA 413; turn left.*

21.2 (0.3) *Hamlet of Buckingham Valley; turn right onto Upper Mountain Road.*

22.5 (1.3) *Junction with Forest Grove Road; turn right.*

23.4 (0.9) *"Y"; bear left on Forest Grove Road.*

23.7 (0.3) *Intersection with PA 263; go straight onto Furlong-Edison Road.*

24.7 (1.0) *Intersection with Pebble Hill Road; turn right.*

26.7 (2.0) *Turn right onto Scout Way and go to the Mercer Museum.*

Bicycle Shops:
Bike Tech, 73 Old Dublin Pike, Mercer Square No. 4, Doylestown, (215) 348-8015

5 Oley Valley

- **Berks County**
- **Start and end at the Daniel Boone Homestead (north of US 422 near Birdsboro)**
- **36.3 miles; flat to rolling with a few climbs**
- **1 day**

In 1734 Oley Valley was on the frontier of American civilization, a fertile area inhabited by pioneering Scotch-Irish and still visited by Indians. Here in a log cabin was born a man whose name conjures up pioneer rigors and adventures. Daniel Boone—explorer, settler, Indian fighter, patriot and leader—grew to young manhood in this southern corner of Berks County.

As a youth, Daniel Boone learned woodcraft and Indian ways from the neighboring Shawnees. When he was not helping his father with farming, weaving, and blacksmithing, he took to the woods. Once he disappeared for several days, alarming his parents. A search party followed a curl of smoke to where young Daniel had built a small cabin and was roasting his evening meal.

From Pennsylvania, Boone moved to North Carolina, then Kentucky, and finally Missouri, always looking for new wilderness to conquer. His daring escapes from the Indians became legendary. Once, when taken by Shawnees, he cleverly cooperated with his captors, obtaining the surrender of others in his party. The Indians adopted him, calling him the chief's son. Then when an opportunity for escape came, he raced 160 miles to warn his settlement, Boonesboro, of an impending Indian attack. On another occasion he escaped pursuing Indians by springing from the edge of a cliff, landing in the branches of a sugar maple, and climbing down to safety in the valley below.

For the most part, though, Daniel Boone was a friend to the Indians. They respected his genuine warmth of heart, they admired his courage, and they valued his honesty. These qualities also helped to make Boone a legendary figure.

0.0 (0.0) *Leaving the Daniel Boone Homestead entrance, turn left onto Daniel Boone Road.*

The DANIEL BOONE HOMESTEAD (9–5 Tues.–Sat., 12–5 Sun.; charge) is not the actual building in which Boone was born. After his family moved to North Carolina the log cabin received a stone addition, and then its logs were replaced from the foundation

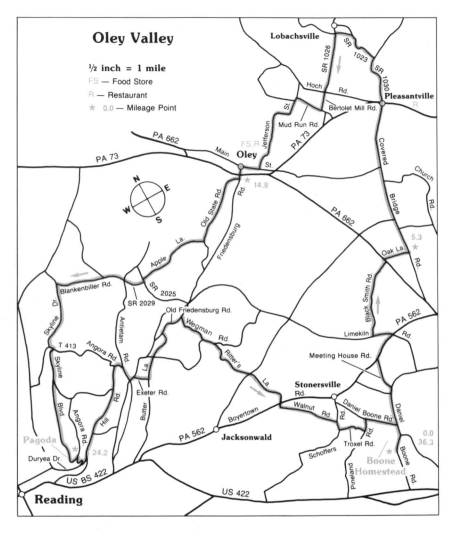

up with stone walls. The cellar of the original cabin with its spring still remains. The whole building has been restored to its late-eighteenth-century appearance and is open for tours.

Surrounding the homestead is a sizeable park with fields and woods bordered by split rail fences. At the entrance is a visitors center, which offers a slide presentation. Near the homestead is a museum, a blacksmith shop, and a Pennsylvania German barn with an assortment of farm animals.

1.5 (1.5) *Immediately after crossing a small stream, turn left onto Meeting House Road.*

1.7 On the right is the EXETER FRIENDS MEETING HOUSE, a one-story stone building of the 1750s. The graveyard contains Boone family members as well as ancestors of Abraham Lincoln. This graveyard is unusual, because in 1818 dirt was added and new graves were placed on top of old ones.

2.1 (0.6) *Junction with PA 562; turn right.*

2.7 (0.6) *Intersection with Limekiln road; turn left.*
Along this road are several huge Pennsylvania barns, with their characteristic forebays or overhangs.

3.1 (0.4) *Turn right onto Black Smith Road.*
    3.9 At the top of the bank on the left is the stone-walled and cedar-flanked Jean Bertolet Graveyard. Bertolet was among the Huguenots, or French Protestants, who sought refuge in Penn's tolerant colony.
    4.2 On the left, far across the valley, can be seen the waste piles of a limestone quarry. The encroachment of these quarries is the Oley Valley's most serious environmental problem.

4.7 (1.6) *Intersection with PA 662; turn left, then immediately right onto Oak Lane.*

5.3 (0.6) *Junction with Covered Bridge Road; turn left.*
    Immediately on the left is a Georgian farmhouse made of cut stone. The barn just beyond it, made of uncut stone, has arched doorways. Stone architecture like this has put Oley Township on the National Register of Historic Places. The valley boasts the heaviest concentration of early stone structures in the United States, as well as the largest collection of eighteenth-century handmade tile roofs.
    6.0 On the right at the spot where Turnpike Road joins from the left is a two-story frame house. This building was formerly a turnpike tollhouse. A pike, or turnstile, would have prevented access to the road until a toll was paid. Commercial tollroads initiated America's road system.
    6.8 Church Road joins on the right.
        Right here 0.5 mile is GREISEMER'S COVERED BRIDGE, built in 1832 and the oldest in the county. Its picturesque setting includes a stone mill and a large white barn.
    8.0 The route crosses the PLEASANTVILLE COVERED BRIDGE, built in 1852. The residence at the end is another former tollhouse.

8.4 (3.1) *Intersection with PA 73 in Pleasantville; go straight on Covered Bridge Road (SR 1030).*

9.5 (1.1) *Turn left onto the road to Lobachsville.*

The route makes a short climb over a hill made of erosion-resistant gneiss and quartzite, with views of the limestone Oley Valley.

10.1 Many of the tombstones at St. Paul's Church have German script on them.

10.2 (0.7) *Left on SR 1023 (main road).*

10.5 (0.3) *Intersection with SR 1026 in Lobachville; turn left.*
Lobachville is a quiet village of stone buildings.

11.8 (1.3) *Intersection with Hoch Road; go straight onto Bertolet Mill Road.*

12.2 (0.4) *Junction with Mud Run Road; turn right.*

12.7 (0.5) *Junction with Jefferson Street; turn left, then immediately left again, continuing on Jefferson Street.*

14.6 (1.9) *Junction with Main Street; turn right into Oley.*

Side by side with little or no front yards, Georgian houses of brick, frame, or stone line OLEY's Main Street. The town, which is also known as Friedensburg, is heavily German as is its surrounding area. On PA 73 at the edge of town, the locally popular Oley Legion Diner serves stuffed noodles, chow-chow, shoofly pie, and other Pennsylvania Dutch delectables.

14.9 (0.3) *Turn left onto Friedensburg Road; then, after crossing PA 73, turn right onto Old State Road.*

16.0 On the right, the Reiff homestead, like others through here, consists of old stone buildings; several of them have orange handmade tile roofs.

16.7 (1.8) *Right onto Apple Lane.*

The route begins a gradual ascent onto the mostly wooded Reading Prong, part of the Blue Ridge of the Appalachians, here more hilly than mountainous.

18.3 (1.6) *Junction with SR 2025 (unmarked); turn left, then immediately right onto SR 2029.*

19.2 (0.9) *"Y"; bear left onto Blankenbiller Road.*

20.3 (1.1) *Junction with Skyline Drive (unmarked); turn left.*

21.7 (1.4) *Junction with T 413 (unmarked); turn left, then immediately right onto Skyline Boulevard (unmarked).*
A steep downslope on the right permits many unhindered views

of the broad GREAT VALLEY of the Appalachians, stretching under one name or another from the St. Lawrence Valley to central Alabama. The basin was formed by the erosion of limestone, shale, and slate. This elevation also offers views to the left of the hilly Reading Prong area.

23.4 On the left is a tall stone tower. Although its Gothic features make it look like part of a castle, it is actually a fire tower built by the Civilian Conservation Corps during the Depression.

24.2 On the edge of the mountain overlooking Reading is the JAPANESE PAGODA, a seven-story building with progressively smaller upturned roofs on each of its top five stories. A torii, or Japanese gateway, stands at the entrance, and an Oriental garden is across the road. Early in this century, a quarry operator built the pagoda to be a luxury hotel, partly because he felt guilty about scarring the mountainside. After the hotel failed, the building was turned over to the city of Reading. The Pagoda holds a restaurant, a gift shop, and a top-floor observation deck and museum.

Almost straight below lies Reading. Lines of row houses with slate and red tin roofs are broken by church steeples and factory smokestacks. The city became an industrial center because of its location on the Schuylkill River, a major coal shipping route, and because of the skilled German artisans who settled here.

A barn built to last in the Oley Valley.

24.4 (2.7) *Right onto Angora Road (unmarked)*
The route begins a switchback descent from Mount Penn.

24.7 (0.3) *Left onto Duryea Drive (unmarked).*

24.8 (0.1) *Junction with Hill Road (unmarked); turn left.*
Gardens, scattered residences, and several ponds are along the route.

27.0 (2.2) *Junction with Angora Road; turn right.*
On the left is manmade Antietam Lake, water source for Mount Penn.

27.2 (0.2) *Junction with Antietam Road; turn right.*

27.5 (0.3) *Intersection with a road to Oley; turn left, then at a "Y" bear right onto Exeter Road.*
The California bungalow, an early 1900s-style house, is common in this section of Mount Penn and identifies it as an early automobile age suburb.

27.9 (0.4) *Junction with Butter Lane; turn left.*
The route continues through a wooded hilly area, eventually descending to the Oley Valley.

29.0 (1.1) *Junction with Old Friedensburg Road; turn right.*

29.6 (0.6) *Right onto Wegman Road.*

30.5 (0.9) *"Y"; bear right onto Ritter's Lane.*

32.7 (2.2) *Intersection with Boyertown Road; go straight onto Walnut Road.*
Along the right side of this lane is a hill rising 200 feet above the countryside. It is made of erosion-resistant volcanic rock which flowed into layers of sedimentary rock that have now disappeared. Volcanic activity occurred during a faulting period after the Appalachians were created.

33.9 (1.2) *Junction with Schoffers Road; turn right, then after 0.2 mile turn left onto Troxel Road.*

34.7 (0.8) *Junction with Pineland Road; turn left, then at the junction with Daniel Boone Road turn right.*

35.6 (0.9) *Junction; turn right on Daniel Boone Road.*

36.3 (0.7) *Daniel Boone Homestead.*

Bicycle Shops:
None on route. The nearest shops are in Birdsboro and Shillington.

6 Hopewell Village

- **Berks and Chester Counties**
- **Start and end at Marsh Creek State Park**
- **31.4 miles; hilly**
- **1 day**

In the early 1800s Hopewell Village was one of hundreds of eastern Pennsylvania iron furnace plantations. Like the tobacco plantations of Virginia, these furnace villages were self-supporting communities oriented to the production of a single commodity. They were agriculturally self-sufficient, too, with grain fields, gardens, orchards, and livestock.

The owner of the furnace (or his appointed ironmaster) lived in a mansion from which he managed the furnace operations. He and his family lived as country gentry with expensive furniture, fine clothing, and household servants.

The village clerk supervised the community store, kept records of employees' earnings and purchases, and managed the routine business transactions of the furnace. An employee called "the founder" was responsible for the operation of the furnace and the quality of the iron produced. Furnace laborers and craftsmen dominated the village population.

In the nearby hills woodcutters chopped the hardwood billets that colliers made into charcoal. On flat round areas in the forest the wood was stacked to form cone-shaped chimneys, covered with leaves and dust to seal out air, and then ignited. During the two weeks that the piles smoldered the colliers lived nearby in sod huts, so they could watch the piles and prevent them from catching fire.

Teamsters brought this charcoal, iron ore, and limestone to a plantation, where workmen labored night and day, pouring the materials in the right proportions into the furnace. Periodically the founder tapped the furnace, draining off molten iron and slag residue. The liquid iron was either ladled into sand molds to make such things as stove parts, or channeled out onto the ground for pig bars to be hammered into objects.

0.0 (0.0) *Leaving the parking lot at the Marsh Creek State Park office, turn right onto Park Road.*

MARSH CREEK STATE PARK is a day-use facility which has a lake and a swimming pool (with showers). The Marsh Creek State Park Youth Hostel (215-458-5881) is across the lake from the park

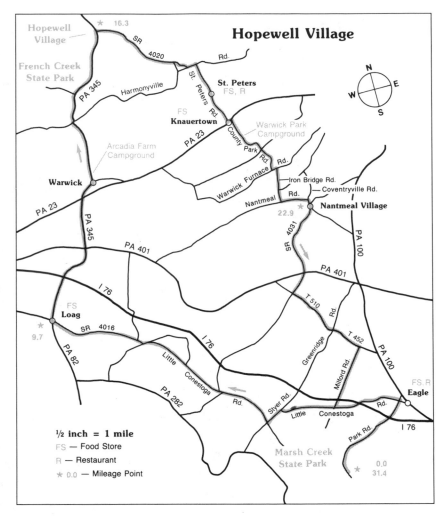

office. In an old farmhouse, this American Youth Hostel offers dormitory sleeping, a kitchen, and social areas. An introductory pass is available for nonmembers.

1.7 (1.7) *Intersection with Little Conestoga Road; turn left.*
    Through here are recent suburban developments, the front line of Philadelphia suburbia, where the backyard lawnmower meets the back-forty manure spreader.

4.3 (2.6) *Junction with Styer Road; turn left.*

4.6 (0.3) *Intersection; turn right onto Little Conestoga Road.*

7.8 (3.2) *"Y"; bear right onto SR 4016.*

Occasional developments interrupt a bucolic setting.

9.7 (1.9) *Intersection in Loag; turn right onto PA 345.*

The crossroads hamlet of Loag's Corner began as a drove stand, where farmers delivered cattle and hogs to Reading butchers.

10.6 Pass over the Pennsylvania Turnpike, America's first modern four-lane highway.

12.9 Warwick was founded when Reverend Levi Bull built St. Mary's Episcopal Church in 1806. The stucco building still stands, although it was rebuilt in 1843. The hamlet took its name from the nearby and famous Warwick Furnace.

14.9 A road to French Creek State Park joins on the left.

On this road 1.3 miles, over fairly level terrain, is the main area of FRENCH CREEK STATE PARK (215-582-1514). Here is the park office, Hopewell Lake, a swimming pool, and a campground with a camp store. The campground is open year-round. It does not accept reservations.

The roadside becomes more wooded as the terrain becomes more hilly.

16.3 (6.6) *Turn right on the road to St. Peters.*

On the left is the entrance to HOPEWELL VILLAGE NATIONAL HISTORIC SITE (9-5 daily except Christmas and New Year's Day; free), the finest existing example of an early American ironmaking community. The Hopewell furnace was constructed in 1771, prospered from 1820-1840, and was finally shut down in 1883. While it operated, the furnace produced a variety of stoves for which it was well known, along with other finished items and pig iron. The federal government purchased the property in 1935 and renovated or reconstructed buildings to return the village to its appearance during its prosperous years. In the summer, costumed interpreters give tours of the buildings. A visitors center offers a slide presentation and exhibits, including several examples of Hopewell stoves.

18.4 (2.1) *Junction with Harmonyville Road; turn left, then after 0.1 mile turn right onto St. Peters Road.*

19.4 The village of ST. PETERS was once a company town for the French Creek Granite Company. The company mined "black granite," a rock of volcanic origin which was used in ornamental and architectural work. Today the Victorian frame buildings hold food, craft, and gift shops, and Muzak plays in the streets.

St. Peters sits alongside the Falls of French Creek, which is actually a drop of the creek through an area full of boulders. The

Kids swimming in French Creek at St. Peter's Village.

rock is the same as that once mined nearby. Paths and bridges criss-cross this scenic glen.

20.0 (1.6) *Junction with PA 23 in Knauertown; turn left, then immediately right onto County Park Road.*

20.5 WARWICK PARK (215-469-9461), a Chester County Park on French Creek, includes woodlands once lumbered to make charcoal for nearby iron furnaces. Trails in the park pass by round, flat areas that were charcoal hearths. The park has picnic and camping areas.

Leaving French Creek Valley, the route passes a number of old stone and stuccoed barns and farmhouses.

21.5 (1.5) *Junction with Warwick Furnace Road; turn left, then after crossing a bridge turn right onto Iron Bridge Road.*

Many of the old farms here belong to wealthy part-time farmers, "the mink-and-manure set."

22.3 (0.8) *Junction with Nantmeal Road; turn left.*

22.9 (0.6) *Junction with Coventryville Road; turn right, then in Nantmeal Village turn right onto SR 4031.*

The route climbs to a small plateau through small sloped fields, woods, and stone and stuccoed structures.

24.4 (1.5) *Intersection with PA 401; go straight on SR 4031.*

25.0 (0.6) *Intersection with T 510 (unmarked); turn left.*

26.2 (1.2) *Intersection with Greenridge Road; go straight onto T 452.*

26.8 (0.6) *Turn right onto Milford Road.*

28.1 (1.3) *Intersection with Conestoga Road; turn left.*

29.6 (1.5) *Intersection with Park Road; turn right.*

31.4 (1.8) *Marsh Creek State Park.*

Bicycle Shops:
None on route. The nearest shops are in Pottstown, Downington, West Chester, and Exton.

7 Dutch Country

- **Lancaster County**
- **Start and end at the Railroad Museum of Pennsylvania (2 miles east of Strasburg on PA 741)**
- **27.8 miles; flat to rolling**
- **1 day**

The Amish trace their heritage to sixteenth century Europe and the Reformation. Martin Luther's reforms were too mild for the Anabaptists, a Protestant splinter group named for their belief in adult, rather than child, baptism. Their dissension brought vicious persecution from both Protestants and Catholics. The courage of Anabaptist leaders in the face of this hostility attracted Menno Simons, a Dutch priest, who became an untiring Anabaptist writer, preacher, and leader. His followers were known as Mennonites.

In the late 1600s Jacob Ammann, a young Mennonite bishop, caused a schism among Swiss Mennonites in Switzerland, Alsace, and Southern Germany. He advocated stricter adherence to certain Mennonite practices such as the *Meidung*, or social avoidance of excommunicates, and the ritual of washing one another's feet, as Christ washed the Apostles' feet. Ammann also attached importance to the wearing of traditional, simple clothing, and to the avoidance of worldly grooming styles. His followers became known as the Amish.

During the seventeenth century the lands along the Rhine, lying between France and the many German states, were subject to the destruction, famine, and pestilence of war. The region's changing politics made followers of certain religions, including the Amish, frequent victims of persecution. In this precarious situation, many Amish quickly accepted William Penn's offer to settle in tolerant and bountiful Pennsylvania.

0.0 (0.0) *Leaving the Railroad Museum of Pennsylvania's parking area, turn left toward Strasburg onto PA 741.*

The RAILROAD MUSEUM OF PENNSYLVANIA (Apr.-Oct. 9–5 Mon.-Sat., 1–5 Sun., Nov.-Mar., closed Mon., closed certain holidays, 717–687–8628; charge), another state museum, holds a collection of steam, diesel, and electric locomotives; various railroad cars including coach, sleeping, and dining cars; and railroad artifacts such as lanterns and uniforms. Visitors are allowed to enter the cab of a steam locomotive and to view the plush stateroom of a private car.

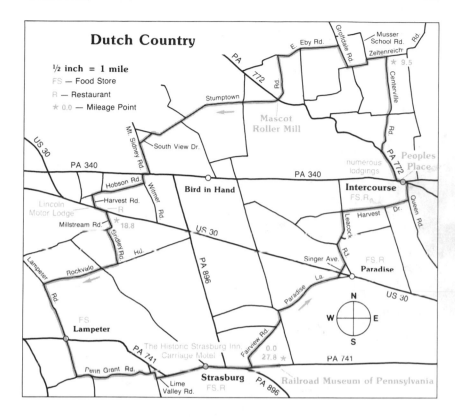

Across the road from the museum is the STRASBURG RAIL-
ROAD (717-687-7522), a private tourist railroad which runs a steam
locomotive through the Lancaster countryside to the town of
Paradise. The round trip takes forty-five minutes.

0.5 (0.5) *Turn right onto Fairview Road.*

1.8 (1.3) *Junction with Paradise Lane; turn left, then at the next
junction turn right onto Paradise Lane.*

The route passes through landscape typical of the Lancaster
Plain: many large white barns, each paired with a metal windmill
and surrounded by expansive fields.

3.4 (1.6) *"Y"; bear left, then at the intersection with US 30 in
Paradise go straight onto Singer Avenue.*

Here the Lincoln Highway, or US 30, follows the course of the
Philadelphia-Lancaster Turnpike, built between 1792 and 1794.
Following McAdam's design, it was one of the first roads in America
to be constructed with a stone base. Later this roadway became the

Pennsylvania Road, connecting Philadelphia and Pittsburgh with a stone-surfaced roadway. The Pennsylvania Road's relatively easy travel made it the route of pioneers, pack trains, and Conestoga wagons bound for the Ohio country.

Paradise, a highway village, was originally a tavern location on the Pennsylvania Road. Its name reflects the area's lush farm-land.

3.7 (0.3) *Junction with Leacock road; turn left.*

4.8 (1.1) *Intersection with Harvest Drive; turn right.*

5.2 Here is an Amish farmstead with a brick farmhouse and a large white wooden barn. A garden is in front of the house and a small orchard is nearby. Amish farm families produce much of their own food.

6.2 (1.4) *Junction with Queen Road; turn left.*

Ahead in a small parking lot is a white outhouse-like building which holds an Amish family's telephone. Some Amish allow phones, but they cannot be in the house because they would connect the family with nonbelievers.

6.6 (0.4) *Junction with PA 772 in Intercourse; turn left.*

The names of towns hereabouts have provided a great deal of fun for those of baser mind. INTERCOURSE was so named be-cause it is at the intersection of the Old Philadelphia Pike (PA 340), one of the early King's Highways, and Newport Road (PA 772). The town is a prime tourist stop in "Pennsylvania Dutch Country" and is filled with tourist businesses. It is also a commercial center for the Amish; hitching rails are provided in front of many buildings.

The PEOPLE'S PLACE (Apr.–Oct. 9:30–9:30 Mon.–Sat., Nov.–Mar. 9:30–4:30 Mon.–Sat.; charge for presentations and exhibits), an interpretive center for the Amish, Mennonites, and Hutterites, offers a slide presentation, exhibits, a book shop, and arts and crafts. Although a bit showy, People's Place is respected for its authenticity.

6.8 (0.2) *Right on PA 772.*

7.4 Amish buggy shop on the left. "No Tourists-No Photos." One of the Amish people's objections to tourists is their snapping of photographs. In addition to making the subjects feel like oddities, photography is specifically forbidden by Amish law. This rule is based on the Bible's prohibition of graven images and its passages concerning a show of vanity.

7.5 (0.7) *"Y"; bear right onto Centerville Road.*

7.6 On the left in the middle of a cow pasture is a small water mill that powers a nearby Amish home's water pump.

8.2 "Horseshoeing, Wheel Hooping, General Repair."

8.3 At an intersection is a one-room Amish schoolhouse. Tourists have been known to disrupt school by peeking into Amish schoolhouses or even bursting into classrooms. Visitors still come to this area believing it to be like Colonial Williamsburg, with people paid to live and dress in the old way.

8.5 The farmhouse on the right is actually three houses end-on-end, one for each generation.

9.1 Phillips Lancaster County Swiss Cheese Company on the right. Cheese is for sale in a small shop.

9.4 On the right is a small dam and water mill. A wire extending from it dangles over the road and attaches to a pump at the farm on the left.

9.5 (2.0) *Junction with Zeltenreich Road; turn left.*

9.9 (0.4) *Junction with Musser School Road; turn left.*

10.4 (0.5) *Right onto Groffdale Road.*

10.7 Beiler's Harness Shop is at the farm on the right.

10.9 (0.5) *Turn left onto East Eby Road.*

An inoffensive way to meet the Amish is to buy some of the homemade products which they sell at their farmhouses or roadside stands.

11.8 On the left is the Myers School, a one-room brick Amish schoolhouse. All Amish children attended public schools until 1938, when the adults began building their own schools. One-room public schools and compulsory attendance in the elementary grades had been acceptable to the Amish. Those schools even helped Amish children learn how to be different in a modern world. But school district consolidation and the building of large schools threatened to remove the children's education from Amish influence. And requirements to attend high school separated youngsters from Amish society during the critical teenage period.

When the Amish refused to send their children to consolidated public high schools, some protesting parents even went to jail. The controversy continued until 1955, when the state allowed an arrangement under which Amish children would attend their own elementary schools. After the eighth grade they could perform farm and household duties under parental guidance, keep a daily journal of their activities, and meet in Amish vocational classes for three hours each week.

11.9 On the right is the Amish Myers Cemetery.

12.2 (1.3) *Turn left onto Stumptown Road.*

13.0 The stone MASCOT ROLLER MILL is a restored grist mill.

13.7 There are stables in the rear of the Stumptown Mennonite Church. They were built when the Mennonites still used horses, and now they hold horses of Amish youths attending Saturday morning vocational sessions at a nearby school.

14.3 The Amish farm on the left stores milk in a gas-run milk cooler before it is shipped by tank truck to a creamery. Stricter Amish transport their milk in traditional milk cans.

15.9 (3.7) *Turn left onto South View Drive.*

16.2 (0.3) *Junction with Mt. Sidney Road; turn left.*

16.9 (0.7) *Junction with PA 340; turn right, then immediately left onto Witmer Road.*

17.2 (0.3) *Turn right onto Hobson Road.*

18.2 (1.0) *Turn left onto Harvest Road.*

18.5 (0.3) *Junction with US 30; turn left, then after 0.3 mile turn right onto Millstream Road.*

An example of the many "grandfather" houses the Amish have built to accommodate two generations of a family.

US 30, a strip of chain restaurants and tourist attractions, is most visitors' impression of Lancaster County. A fiberglass Amish couple stands by their buggy in front of Howard Johnson's. "The Amish Village" explains Amish life even though the Amish do not live in villages.

On Millstream Road is the Mennonite Information Center. Mennonite staff members here are friendly and knowledgable. The center offers literature, displays, and a free film about the Mennonites.

19.2 (0.7) *Turn left onto Gridley Road.*

19.8 On the left is Glick's Buggy Shop. Most Amish still use horses for transportation, although for long trips they may use public transportation or have friends or paid drivers transport them by automobile. The use of horses, the prohibition of electricity, and dress requirements are prescribed in the *Ordnung,* a set of regulations determined by the leaders of each church district. Some of the rules have direct biblical support; others do not. Their objects are to protect Amish members from worldliness and to keep them separate from nonbelievers. The rules are basically the same from one church district to the next, but slight variations occur. For instance, grey is the predominant buggy top color in Lancaster County, but black, white, and yellow tops are prescribed in other places.

19.9 (0.7) *Junction with Rockvale Road; turn right.*

21.5 (1.6) *Junction with Lampeter Road; turn left.*

21.9 The hamlet of Lampeter took its name from Peter Yeordy, an early settler who was lame.

23.5 (2.0) *Where the main road goes right, turn left onto Penn Grant Road.*

23.8 (0.3) *"Y"; bear left on Penn Grant Road.*

24.3 The route crosses a covered bridge.

25.4 (1.6) *After a bend to the right, turn left onto Lime Valley Road, then go straight at the junction with PA 741 into Strasburg.*

In its early days STRASBURG, a village of brick Georgian houses, was a halting place for Conestoga wagons and stage coaches. It had as many as ten hotels offering "entertainment for man or beast," but no churches. For this reason Strasburg was known as Hell Hole.

27.8 (2.4) *Railroad Museum of Pennsylvania.*

Bicycle Shops:
None on the route. The nearest shops are in Lancaster and Leola.

8 Ephrata

- **Lancaster County**
- **Start and end at Pennsylvania Farm Museum of Landis Valley (off PA 272 at Landis Valley)**
- **29.7 miles; mostly flat, occasionally rolling**
- **1 day**

In 1728 Conrad Beissel, a German religious exile, began living as a hermit on Cocalico Creek where the town of Ephrata now stands. His observance of the Sabbath on the seventh day, rather than the first, had caused him to break with his Lancaster County Dunker (or German Baptist) congregation. But Beissel soon attracted followers who wished to live under his guidance, and a community of ascetics formed. These Seventh-Day German Baptists organized as three orders: a Brotherhood, a Sisterhood, and a congregation of married couples.

Every part of life at the Ephrata cloister was ordered to instill the Christian virtues of humility, chastity, temperance, fortitude, and charity. The low doorways of their buildings required constant stooping to remind them of humility, and their long narrow passageways recollected the "straight and narrow path." The celibate brothers and sisters lived in small dormitory cells, slept on uncomfortably short wooden ledges with wooden blocks for pillows, and ate plain and meager food. Two three-hour rest periods were allowed each day—the first from nine to midnight (when all were roused for prayer), the second from one to four in the morning.

Both work and its proceeds were shared by cloister members. The sisters busied themselves with indoor crafts such as quilting, basketry, drawing, and canning. The farming and heavier outside work were left to the brothers, as were shoemaking, weaving, and tailoring. The results of the community's labors—especially its publishing, artwork, and music—won widespread fame.

After the death of Conrad Beissel, the Ephrata Cloister began to decline. It had grown from a hut on Cocalico Creek to an institution of international reputation. But the growing young country was oriented to more worldly pursuits. Early in the nineteenth century the few remaining members of the Brotherhood and Sisterhood turned the cloister over to the congregation. The congregation dissolved in 1934.

0.0 (0.0) *Leaving the Pennsylvania Farm Museum's parking lot, turn left onto Landis Valley Road.*

The PENNSYLVANIA FARM MUSEUM OF LANDIS VALLEY (9-5 Tues.–Sat., 12-5 Sun., closed certain holidays, 717-569-0401; charge) is one of Pennsylvania's fine state museums. The twenty-two buildings, some of which are relocated historic structures, hold exhibits of the state's rural past. Farm homes include a German settler's cabin and a Victorian farmhouse. Most of the buildings are village shops—the blacksmith shop, the gun shop, and the pottery shop. Others include a one-room schoolhouse and a tavern. Throughout the complex, costumed employees give demonstrations of rural crafts such as weaving and harness making.

1.0 (1.0) *Intersection with Butter Road; turn left.*

Slow-moving CONESTOGA CREEK flows along the right. Craftsmen in this valley made the massive Conestoga wagon, which carried America west.

1.8 (0.8) *Intersection with Hunsicker Road; turn right.*

2.4 The route crosses Conestoga Creek on a covered bridge.

2.7 (0.9) *Intersection with Mondale Road; turn left.*

2.9 The white outhouse-like building in front of a brick farmhouse holds a private telephone for the Amish family that lives here.

Here in the limestone lowland of the Lancaster plain, the views are of expansive fields with many large white wooden barns.

4.0 (1.3) *Junction with Snake Hill Road; turn right, then immediately left onto Stormstown Road.*

Large leafy tobacco plants are cultivated here in fields alternating with corn fields. Tobacco saps the soil's fertility and must be rotated with other crops.

4.8 (0.8) *Junction with Quarry Road; turn right.*

5.0 (0.2) *Left onto Center Square Road.*

The gentle landscape is punctuated with metal windmills and water pumps for farmers.

5.4 (0.4) *Junction; turn right onto Center Square Road.*

7.6 Here is a white, one-room Amish schoolhouse with a bell mounted on top. At the back of the lot is a typical pair of outhouses.

7.8 (2.4) *Left onto Brethren Church Road.*

8.1 The Amish farmhouse here has a house attached to it. This is a "grandfather" house where a retired Amish couple can live independently but close to their children.

8.6 (0.8) *Junction with West Farmersville Road; turn right.*

9.5 (0.9) *Intersection with North Farmersville Road in Farmersville; turn left.*

9.9 (0.4) *Right onto Covered Bridge Road.*

11.1 (1.2) *Junction; turn left over a covered bridge onto Cider Mill Road.*

11.5 (0.4) *Junction with Willis Pierce Road; turn left and continue around bend onto Pearshing Weeg Road.*

11.8 Here is another one-room Amish schoolhouse.

12.6 (1.1) *Junction with Diamond Station Road; turn right, then immediately left onto East Fulton Street.*

12.7 Ephrata Mountain, the low wooded hill ahead, is made of quartz-sandstone conglomerate, a more resistant rock than the limestone that over the ages has worn away around it.

14.6 (2.0) *Intersection with South Oak Street in Ephrata; turn left.*

Conrad Beissel gave EPHRATA its name, an old designation for the biblical city of Bethlehem. Today its small business section is filled with German merchant names: Musser, Kreter, Sprecher. Mennonite men with black hats and suspenders and Mennonite women with caps and plain dresses are among the shoppers. As in other Pennsylvania German towns, textile production is an important industry.

The EPHRATA CLOISTER (9-5 Mon.–Sat., 12-5 Sun., closed certain holidays, 717-733-6600; charge) is on West Main Street. (From the route, continue straight at South Oak Street, then turn left on Main Street.) On the grounds among walnut and locust trees are ten of the original buildings, which have medieval German features such as steep roofs with shed dormers and small unbalanced windows. The structures have been returned to their eighteenth-century appearance. *Vorspiel,* a musical drama depicting eighteenth-century cloister life, is presented at dusk on Saturdays throughout the summer.

The Ephrata Cloister.

16.0 The white building across from the farmhouse is a tobacco barn. Slats on its sides open to allow air movement.

17.8 (3.2) *Intersection with Middle Creek Road; turn right.*

19.2 (1.4) *After a bend to the right, turn left onto Brubaker Road.*
Many of the Amish sell such things as produce, baked goods, and homemade root beer at stands along the road or at their farmhouses. Homemade signs at mail boxes are common along these back roads.

19.8 (0.6) *Junction with Buch Mill Road; turn right, then left at a junction with Lincoln Road.*

20.6 (0.8) *"Y"; bear right to continue on Lincoln Road.*

21.1 (0.5) *Junction with Clay Road; turn left, then immediately right on Lincoln Road.*

22.0 (0.9) *Junction with Brunnerville Road in Brunnerville; turn left.*

23.7 (1.7) *"Y"; bear left, then immediately turn left onto North Locust Street.*

24.3 (0.6) *Intersection with East Main Street in Lititz; go straight onto South Locust Street.*
To the right on maple-lined Main Street is the attractive business section of LITITZ, its fountain and square surrounded by eighteenth-century buildings, some of which bear Victorian alterations. The people of Lititz have taken pains to preserve the old charm of their community: old-fashioned facades and wooden signs mark the commercial establishments. Near the square a small park holds Lititz Spring, a large limestone spring, once a watering hole for the Indians. The Wilbur Chocolate Company fills the town with its sweet smell.

Moravian missionaries laid out Lititz in 1757 and named it for a barony in Moravia. Originally they controlled both religious and secular interests in the town. Around the MORAVIAN CHURCH SQUARE, a grassy area, are a number of early Moravian buildings, including the spired Moravian church, built in 1788. One-story eighteenth-century homes are spread throughout the older part of town. A good example is the JOHANNES MUELLER HOUSE (717-626-7958) which holds a collection of Lititz artifacts and has several authentically furnished rooms.

The STURGIS PRETZEL HOUSE (9-5 Mon.–Sat., closed winter holidays; charge) at 219 East Main Street has been a bakery since

1784. In 1861 it became the first pretzel bakery in the United States after Julius Sturgis gave a hobo a meal in exchange for a pretzel recipe. In addition to selling pretzels in its store (along with assorted Pennsylvania Dutch trinkets), the company gives tours of its small bakery. A modest admission fee buys a ticket (a pretzel) for the tour, which provides an animated explanation of pretzel history and a chance to twist a pretzel (certificates awarded).

Also in Lititz is the CANDY AMERICANA MUSEUM (10–5 Mon.–Sat.; free) at the Wilbur Chocolate Factory. The museum holds a collection of candy manufacturing equipment and utensils. It is part of a factory outlet store.

On the square in Lititz is the General Sutter Inn (717-616-2115), a descendent of the Zum Auker Inn established there by the Moravian Church in 1764. In its early days, the inn was known for its unique feather beds, heated rooms, and the innkeeper's prohibition of dancing, cursing, gossip, and bawdy songs. The building went under several structural changes before it became the three-story brick building it is today. The inn has a coffee shop, restaurant, and rooms (with or without baths), all elaborately furnished in Victorian decor.

24.6 (0.3) *"Y"; bear left onto Kissel Hill Road.*

25.2 (0.6) *Junction with Owl Hill Road; turn right.*

25.7 (0.5) *Intersection with Landis Valley Road; turn left.*

26.8 (1.1) *Turn right onto Kissel Hill Road.*

27.2 (0.4) *Junction with Millport Road; turn right, then immediately left onto Kissel Hill Road.*

29.6 (2.4) *Junction with Valley Road; go right 0.1 mile to the Pennsylvania Farm Museum.*

Bicycle Shops:
Bicycle World, 747 South Broad Street, Lititz, (717) 626-0650
Martin's Bicycle Shop, R.D. 3, Ephrata, (717) 354-9127

9 Lower Susquehanna

- **York and Lancaster Counties**
- **Start and end at Columbia**
- **55.2 miles; hilly with some climbs, a few steep**
- **1 or 2 days; overnight stop at Otter Creek Campground (mile 36.3)**

With humble beginnings in Otsego Lake near Cooperstown, New York, the Susquehanna River stretches 444 miles. On its way it bisects eastern Pennsylvania, gathering the waters of the Chemung, West Branch, and Juniata, then flows into Maryland where it meets saltwater in the Chesapeake Bay. "Susquehanna" is a combination of two Indian words: *sisku,* meaning mud, and *hanne,* meaning river. Long ago the banks of the river and its tributaries were crossed by Indian trails, and the streams themselves carried Indian bark and dugout canoes. Early settlers followed the river's path, using its water gaps to penetrate mountain barriers. In 1771 the river was declared a public highway, but only very shallow vessels could navigate it until the early 1800s, when canals were built along its shores. In time, railroads followed, and they in turn were paralleled by highways.

With the benefit of transportation, towns flourished along the Susquehanna's banks, capitalizing on agriculture, lumber, and coal. With this came civilization's wastes: erosion, sewage, acid mine drainage, chemicals, and other industrial pollutants. Mine operators would wash their coal, dumping so much sediment into the river that, well into the 50s, dredging the muddy bottoms for coal was a profitable business. In recent years, however, stricter environmental controls, including Pennsylvania's clean stream law, have cleared up the waterway and made the river a haven for fishermen once again.

0.0 (0.0) *Intersection of PA 462 and PA 441 in Columbia; head south on PA 441.*

On the banks of the Susquehanna River, COLUMBIA is a small town with interesting nineteenth-century architecture. It was settled in 1726 and soon became well known because of John Wright's ferry. In fact, the location was seriously considered for the nation's capital.

Columbia was a key river crossing during the 1800s (before the Battle of Gettysburg, Union troops burned its covered bridge to prevent the Confederates from reaching Philadelphia). In 1834 the

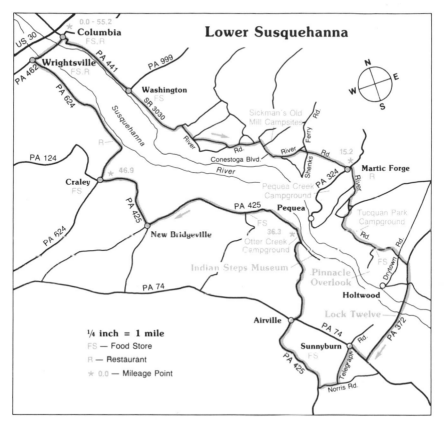

town's position brought the Philadelphia and Columbia Railroad. Lumber rafting and canal traffic also enriched the community.

The stone Georgian WRIGHT FERRY MANSION (May–Oct., 10-3 Tues., Wed., Fri., and Sat.; charge) was built by John Wright in 1726. Located at 38 South Second Street, it has been restored and furnished with period articles. Another place of interest is the town's market hall, where farmers' markets are held on Friday and Saturday. The community also has a pleasant shaded park along the river.

Leaving Columbia, PA 441 passes through farmland with the wide placid Susquehanna on the right, its edges filled with a lush growth of reeds, cattails, and other aquatic plants, the home of egrets, herons, ducks, and geese.

3.6 (3.6) *In Washington, where PA 999 joins on the left, go straight onto SR 3030.*

WASHINGTON, a village on the east bank of the river, was an

Indian trading center in the 1700s and a raftsmen's haven in the 1800s. During the 1830s it had fourteen hotels for river travelers. Now the community is oriented to agriculture, with tobacco and tomatoes its chief crops.

4.6 The white wooden building on the left is a tobacco barn. Vertical slats on the sides open to allow ventilation.

The route leaves the gentle limestone lowlands of the Lancaster Plain and enters an area of old crystalline rock which makes a more rugged terrain. Although it is known as River Road, the road departs from the river at this point to travel through the uplands area, providing views at various points of the river valley.

6.7 (3.1) *Turn right onto the road to Lake Aldred Recreation Areas.*

7.4 (0.7) *"Y"; bear left on River Road.*

10.2 (2.8) *Junction with Conestoga Boulevard; turn right.*

Here is CONESTOGA CREEK PARK, a shaded picnic area along rippling Conestoga Creek.

The route continues through a sparsely populated wooded area.

12.9 (2.7) *"Y"; bear right on River Road.*

13.2 (0.3) *Intersection with Shenks Ferry Road; go straight on River Road.*

15.2 (2.0) *Junction with PA 324 in Martic Forge; turn left across a bridge, then turn right on River Road.*

Right on PA 324 1.1 miles is Pennsylvania Power and Light's PEQUEA CREEK CAMPGROUND AND RECREATION AREA (717-284-4587). The campground has hot showers and a camp-store. Camping is allowed year-round, although in winter certain facilities may be closed down.

16.7 (1.5) *"Y"; bear left on River Road.*

17.1 (0.4) *"Y"; bear right on River Road.*

17.6 (0.5) *"Y"; bear left on River Road.*

The hills here are a patchwork of woodlots, fields dotted with farms, and the homes of dam workers.

19.8 Pinnacle Road joins on the right.

Right here 1.4 miles is the PINNACLE OVERLOOK with a high view of Lake Aldred, a dammed section of the Susquehanna River. Trail maps for various hiking trails in the area are available at the site. The Pinnacle Trail leads to Kellys Run, a scenic gorge.

20.1 Intersection with Drytown Road.

Right here 0.3 mile is the HOLTWOOD ARBORETUM, with 43 tree species, many natural to the area. A picnic area is adjacent.

Left here 0.3 mile is TUCQUAN VINEYARD (717-284-2221), with a shop and wine-tasting room. The wine is made from grapes of nearby vineyards.

20.3 (2.7) *Intersection with PA 372; turn right.*

21.8 From the Norman Wood Bridge are views left and right of the rocky CONOWINGO ISLANDS which practically fill the river and are the erosional remnants of old metamorphic rock—rock which was changed under pressure when the Appalachians were formed. On the right is the Holtwood Dam, a hydroelectric facility.

22.6 On the right is the LOCK TWELVE HISTORIC AREA, with the remnants of a Susquehanna and Tidewater Canal lock. The canal, which was completed in 1839, followed the river. Also here are a restored lime kiln and the remains of a sawmill and pond.

24.7 (4.4) *Junction with PA 74; turn right.*

25.5 (0.8) *Intersection with Telegraph Road in Sunnyburn; turn left.*

The terrain now becomes flatter, and the farmland more prosperous.

26.3 The speaker mounted on a telephone pole here is a siren to warn residents of problems at the nearby Peach Bottom Nuclear Power Plant. Sirens are placed within one mile of each other in a ten-mile radius of the plant.

View of the Susquehanna River from the Pinnacle Overlook.

27.2 (1.7) *Junction with Norris Road; turn right.*

28.1 (0.9) *Junction with PA 425; turn right.*
On this rolling high farmland are views to the east of the wooded Susquehanna Valley.

35.8 At a junction is the site of York Furnace, formerly an iron furnace plantation of the mid-1800s, now a cottage community on Lake Aldred. A stone schoolhouse and a canal warehouse remain from the early settlement.

Right at this junction 0.8 mile is the INDIAN STEPS MUSEUM (717-862-3948), a structure whose exterior is ornamented with the figures of Indians and wildlife formed by arrowheads and other Indian pieces set in concrete. It was built by John Vandersloot and it holds his large collection of Indian artifacts.

On the grounds of this museum, near the banks of the Susquehanna, is an American holly tree of immense size. At a ceremony each year a sprig from the tree is presented to the Great Fathers of Pennsylvania Power and Light as rental for the land.

36.3 On the left is PP & L's OTTER CREEK CAMPGROUND AND RECREATION AREA (717-862-3628). The campground has hot showers and a camp store. It is bordered on one side by the Susquehanna River and on another by Otter Creek, a river tributary with trails, huge hemlocks and tulip poplars, and several waterfalls with pools.

PA 425 climbs steeply from the river and returns to rolling farmland.

46.9 (18.8) *Junction with PA 624 in Craley; turn right.*
PA 624 returns to and follows the Susquehanna, passing cottages and marinas along the shoreline and broken-down remnants of the canal.

50.1 KLINES RUN PARK offers picnicking and swimming in the river.

53.6 (6.7) *Turn left onto PA 462 East in Wrightsville.*
Wrightsville, once the other terminus of Wrights ferry, is now joined to Columbia by a mile-long concrete bridge which formerly carried US 30.

55.2 (1.6) *Columbia.*

Bicycle Shops:
None on route. The nearest shops are in York and Lancaster.

10 Gettysburg

- **Adams County**
- **Start and end at Gettysburg**
- **35.7 miles; flat to rolling with some hills and one climb**
- **1 day**

When, on June 3, 1863, General Robert E. Lee drew his troops from Fredericksburg, Virginia and headed north through the Shenandoah Valley, he had several goals in mind. By bringing the war to the North he hoped to move the fighting out of the South and to encourage Northern peace groups in their efforts to negotiate a settlement. Lee thought his offensive might also win the support of foreign powers.

The Army of the Potomac had been battling Lee in Virginia. When its leaders realized Lee's plan, this Union army also headed north, shielded from Lee by the Blue Ridge Mountains. By the end of June, Lee had reached Cashtown Pass near Gettysburg, where in a good defensive position he decided to wait for the Union army, then headed by General George Meade.

A chance meeting of opposing scouting parties in Gettysburg and later skirmishes there drew the two armies from nearby locations. On July first there was fighting to the north and west of Gettysburg. By the end of the day the Union army was forced to retreat to a position south of Gettysburg. This was Cemetery Ridge and its adjoining areas, a good defensive site which Meade held through the remainder of the battle. The South took a parallel ridge a mile away.

Through the night of July first, the bulk of Meade's army arrived at Gettysburg. On the next day Lee attacked the right and left flanks of the strengthened Union position, but he made only modest gains. When the day ended, Lee concluded that the Union strength lay in its flanks, and that an attack on the center could divide the enemy forces and win the battle. Meade and his generals, speculating on Lee's next move, guessed it would be a frontal charge.

At about one o'clock in the afternoon on July third, Lee's gunners began a massive barrage of the Union line. Meade's cannons answered back for two hours, but then slackened to cool. Misinterpreting this pause as weakening, 12,000 Rebel troops moved forward across open ground to attack the Union front line. Almost immediately the disaster of Pickett's Charge was realized. In a short while 8,000 soldiers lay dead on the field.

Late in the afternoon of July fourth, Lee began an orderly

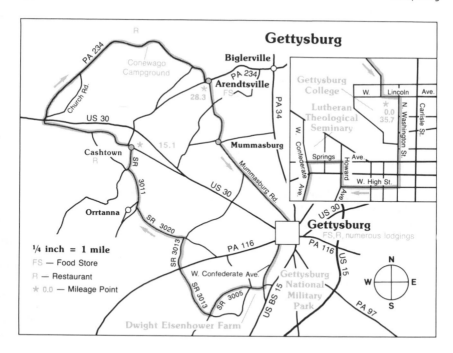

retreat. A seventeen-mile-long wagon train of wounded started home through Cashtown Pass. At night able-bodied men headed to the Potomac by the Hagerstown Road. Lee left, never again to take his army into the North.

0.0 (0.0) *West Lincoln Avenue and North Washington Street at Gettysburg College; turn south onto North Washington Street.*

GETTYSBURG COLLEGE, a small private liberal arts college, has an attractive 200-acre, tree-shaded campus on the north side of Gettysburg. Pennsylvania Hall, built in 1837 and the first college building constructed, is a white-painted brick structure with a pedimented, columned portico and other Greek Revival features. It was used as a field hospital for both the Confederate and Union armies during the Battle of Gettysburg.

The town of GETTYSBURG, seat of Adams County, was founded by James Gettys, who built a hotel and residence there sometime before 1783. In the 1860s it had 2,400 residents, carriage and shoe-making industries, Gettysburg College, and the Lutheran Theological Seminary. Today Gettysburg's economy is strongly dependent on battlefield tourism. It is a large town with a prominent central market square and many fine examples of nineteenth-century architecture.

South of the town lies GETTYSBURG NATIONAL MILITARY PARK, where the major part of the battle took place. Much of the battlefield has been kept as it was at the time of the battle. Modern farmers grow crops that grew there in 1863. Soon after the battle the Gettysburg Battlefield Memorial Association was formed. This group established the park, installed monuments, and built lanes. The federal government purchased the land in 1895, and today the park covers more than twenty-five square miles.

The battlefield VISITORS CENTER (8-6 daily except Thanksgiving, Christmas, and New Years Day; charge for Electric Map), on the edge of Gettysburg opposite the National Cemetery, holds a large collection of Civil War artifacts and the Electric Map, a large floor map with colored lights which show positions and movements of the Union and Confederate armies during the battle.

Adjacent to the visitors center, is the CYCLORAMA CENTER, (open 9 5 daily except Thanksgiving, Christmas, and New Years Day; charge), housing a circular painting, twenty-six feet high and 356 feet in circumference, of Pickett's Charge. It was painted by Paul Philippoteax in 1884.

The Cyclorama, a 356-foot circular painting of Pickett's Charge.

The NATIONAL CEMETERY was established by Pennsylvania Governor Andrew Curtin, who had visited the site only days after the battle and witnessed the difficulties local residents had in attending to the dead. Land was purchased by Pennsylvania and laid out in lots for each state that had lost soldiers. Today the seventeen-acre cemetery is the final resting place of 3,722 Union soldiers as well as of United States veterans from later wars.

On November 19, 1863, Abraham Lincoln delivered the Gettysburg Address at the Gettysburg National Cemetery during its dedication ceremony. The President was not originally invited, since the cemetery was not federal property, but when his interest was discovered, he was asked to speak. The ceremony's main speaker was a famous orator who spoke for two hours. Later, Lincoln remarked that his own short speech "fell like a wet blanket" on the attending crowds.

0.6 (0.6) *Intersection with West High Street; turn right.*

0.9 (0.3) *Junction with South Howard Avenue; turn right, then after two blocks turn left onto Springs Avenue.*

Springs Avenue passes through the LUTHERAN THEOLOGICAL SEMINARY, a group of red brick buildings overlooking the town. The Old Dorm is a three-story red brick structure built in 1832. Its central cupola served as the Confederates' chief signal station. This building was also used as a hospital for both sides.

1.3 (0.4) *Intersection with West Confederate Avenue; turn left.*

West Confederate Avenue lies on top of SEMINARY RIDGE, the main Confederate battle line. The road passes many cannons and memorials.

2.5 THE VIRGINIA MEMORIAL on the left marks the spot where General Robert E. Lee watched 12,000 of his men attempt to break the center of Union lines in Pickett's Charge. When he realized the failure of the attack, he rode out to meet the returning soldiers. "All this has been my fault," he said to General Wilcox who had brought off his command after heavy losses. "It is I that have lost this fight, and you must help me out of it in the best way you can."

Seminary Ridge, Cemetery Ridge, and the Round Tops—all key positions during the battle—are topographic features of former molten rock which flowed into the red sandstones and shales of the Gettysburg Valley 180 million years ago. The sedimentary rock has partially worn away, leaving these harder rock features.

3.4 (2.1) *Intersection with SR 3005; turn right.*

Straight ahead is a lookout tower giving views of the battlefield and of the DWIGHT EISENHOWER FARM (Feb.–Dec. 9-5 daily, limited winter hours). The Eisenhower farm is open to visitors; it can only be reached by shuttle bus from the battlefield visitors center.

4.7 At this highway bridge, the SACHS MILL COVERED BRIDGE is visible on the left. It is a lattice-covered bridge built in 1854.

The route passes through an area of large white barns surrounded by slightly rolling fields of corn and hay.

6.2 (2.8) *Intersection; turn right onto SR 3013.*

The several wooded elevations here mark other ancient lava flows. Volcanic activity occurred during a period of geologic faulting after the building of the Appalachian Mountains.

8.5 (2.3) *Intersection with PA 116; go straight on SR 3013.*

PA 116 is the Hagerstown Road, the retreat route of Lee and his able-bodied soldiers on July 4, 1863. The Union army pursued, but the Confederates had the advantage of a more direct route and were able to escape.

Near this intersection is the Lower Marsh Creek Presbyterian Church, built of stone in 1790.

10.0 (1.5) *Junction with SR 3020; turn left towards Ortanna.*

12.4 (2.4) *Junction with SR 3011; turn right.*

Northern Adams County is the state's most important fruit-growing region. The industry benefits from volcanic rock soils and from South Mountain's slopes, which allow good air drainage, thereby reducing the likelihood of frosts. South Mountain also provides some protection from cold northwest winds.

At this junction is Knouse Foods, one of this fruit-growing region's food processors. Apple and peach growing on the southern slopes of South Mountain began at the turn of the century. A local grower started the industry after he visited the 1893 Chicago World's Fair and learned about transportation technology.

14.1 (1.7) *Junction; turn right on SR 3011 toward Cashtown.*

The route passes through an area thick with apple and peach orchards. The lines of trees over this rolling landscape make a pleasant spectacle, especially when they are blossoming in the spring.

15.1 (1.0) *Junction in Cashtown; turn left onto old route 30.*

The village of CASHTOWN, which lies in the shadow of Rock Top, a steep-sided knob, was supposedly named for an early tavern keeper's insistence that all patrons pay cash. The community was settled as a toll gate on the Gettysburg and Chambersburg Pike, built in 1813. The brick Cashtown Tavern, still operating and still refusing to sell drinks on credit, dates to the early days of the pike.

The route enters CASHTOWN PASS of South Mountain. Here Lee waited for the Union army before the Battle of Gettysburg. And through here passed the wagon train of wounded Confederates on its way south. Brigadier General John O. Imboden, whose cavalry protected the train, recalled later: "During this one night I realized more of the horrors of war than I had in all the two preceding years. From almost every wagon for miles issued heartrending wails of agony. For hours I hurried on my way to the front, and in all that time I was never out of hearing of the groans and cries of the wounded and dying."

19.0 (3.9) *Intersection with US 30; go straight onto PA 234.*

PA 234 passes through Buchanon Valley, a long shallow crease in SOUTH MOUNTAIN. South Mountain, or the Carlisle Prong, is part of the Blue Ridge but is less rugged than other parts such as the Smokies. The period of faulting that included volcanic activity also down-faulted, or dropped, the old bedrock over a wide area of southeastern Pennsylvania, making a lowlands area to the south and diminishing this once great mountain.

21.6 Church Road joins on the right.

On Church Road 0.5 mile is the CHURCH OF ST. IGNATIUS LOYOLA, a brick building erected in 1817 on the site of a Jesuit mission. Nearby is a statue of Mary Jemison, the "white woman of the Genesee," who, with her parents and neighbors, was captured by Indians in the 1750s. Adopted by the Indians, she married a Delaware chief.

PA 234 climbs to a wide ridge with views, then descends through occasional white pine groves to THE NARROWS, the water gap of Conewago Creek. The stream takes a rocky course through thick hemlock and is paralled by the highway.

27.2 SOUTH MOUNTAIN FAIRGROUNDS is on the left. Here on the first Sunday in May is the Apple Blossom Festival and, during the first two weekends of October, the National Apple Harvest Festival. The fall event features craft demonstrations, a variety of apple foods, and the crowning of the Apple Queen, who is, of course, the apple of everyone's eye.

28.3 (9.3) *Arendtsville; turn left onto Main Street, then after one block turn right onto the road to Gettysburg.*

ARENDTSVILLE, with brick Georgian houses, brick sidewalks, and the small front yards typical of Southeastern Pennsylvania villages, is a quiet community which was founded in 1806 by John Arendt.

31.2 (2.9) *Mummasburg; go straight onto Mummasburg Road.*

34.6 On the left is the ETERNAL LIGHT PEACE MEMORIAL, a forty-foot shaft of Alabama limestone topped with a bronze urn. This Civil War monument is in the area of the first day's fighting. It was dedicated by President Franklin D. Roosevelt in 1938 at the last reunion of Civil War Veterans.

35.6 (4.4) *Junction with West Lincoln Avenue; turn left and proceed one block to an intersection with North Washington Street at Gettysburg College.*

Bicycle Shops:
Lawver's Bicycle Shop, 280 Barlow St., Gettysburg, (717) 334-3295

North Ridge and Valley

One after another, long wooded ridges alternate with broad farming valleys, making a corrugated landscape. Because the ridges generally run parallel to the coast and often rise 1,000 feet above valley floors, they made formidable barriers for westward-moving settlers, who sourly named the area the Endless Mountains. Fortunately for them (and for later canals, railroads, and highways), the ridges are occasionally broken by gaps where streams pass through.

Millions upon millions of years ago, Pennsylvania was a shallow sea filling up with layers of sediments: sometimes mud, sometimes sand, sometimes the shells of marine animals. When Africa bumped into North America, the 200-million-year-long collision squeezed and crumpled the rock layers, deforming them most near the coast, but only wrinkling them in the Ridge and Valley Region.

Over many ages this furrowed surface was worn by erosion to a gently sloping plain, which then rose under geologic forces, causing erosion to begin again. Several upliftings and subsequent wearing-downs removed rock to a depth of five miles. Today's landscape of ridges and valleys is the result of a roughly zigzag pattern of rock layers on the last plain's surface, and the wearing away of weaker layers (limestones and shales), which left harder layers (sandstones and quartzites) as ridges. Major streams which ran across the plain kept their courses, cutting water gaps in the ridges.

Lush valley farmlands hemmed in by wooded ridges, and towns of close-spaced Georgian houses characterize the scenery of the Ridge and Valley Region. Valley floors and watergaps make easy bicycle riding, but ridge crossings may sometimes require a two-mile climb. The area has many little-used back roads, and many of the state highways do not have much traffic.

For More Information:
Berks County Visitors Information Association, Sheraton Berkshire Inn, Route 422 West, Paper Mill Road Exit, Wyomissing, PA 19610, (215) 375-4085
Centre County Lion Country Visitors and Convention Bureau, 131 Fraser Street, Plaza 3, State College, PA 16801, (814) 231-1400
Columbia-Montour Tourist Promotion Agency, R.D. 2, Box 109, Bloomsburg, PA 17815, (717) 784-8279
Harrisburg-Hershey-Carlisle Tourism and Convention Bureau, 114 Walnut Street, P.O. Box 969, Harrisburg, PA 17108, (717) 232-1377
Lebanon Valley Tourist and Visitors Bureau, P.O. Box 626, Lebanon, PA 17042, (717) 272-8555
Lehigh Valley Convention and Visitors Bureau, Terminal Building, P.O. Box

2605, Lehigh Valley, PA 18001, (215) 266-0560

Juniata-Mifflin County Tourist Promotion Agency, 3 Monument Square, Suite 104, Lewistown, PA 17044, (717) 248-6713

Perry County Tourist and Recreation Bureau, 23 Cook Road, Duncannon, PA 17020, (717) 834-4912

Susquehanna Valley Visitors Bureau, Courtyard Offices, Suite 270, Box 2, Route 11-15, Selinsgrove, PA 17870, (800) 458-4748

Area Bicycle Clubs:

Berks County Bicycle Club, P.O. Box 8264, Reading, PA 19603

Harrisburg Bicycle Club, 16 East Green Street, Shiremanstown, PA 17011

Lebanon Valley Bicycle Club, 380 Summit Court, Lebanon, PA 17042

Lehigh Wheelmen Association, P.O. Box 356, Bethlehem, PA 18016

Penn State Outing Club, Bicycle Division, 207 Hammond Building, University Park, PA 16802. Sells a bicycle guide for Central Pennsylvania.

State College Bicycling Club, P.O. Box 1173, State College, PA 16804

Susquehanna Valley Bicycle Club, P.O. Box 63, Berwick, PA 18603

Rural farm scene in the Big Valley.

11 Trexlertown

- **Berks and Lehigh Counties**
- **Start and end at Trexlertown Velodrome
  (off U.S. 222 at Trexlertown)**
- **45.2 miles; rolling with some hills**
- **1 day**

Bordering the Great Valley, Blue Mountain is the easternmost of the folded Appalachians in Pennsylvania. This forest-covered sandstone ridge extends nearly the entire length of the Appalachians from Shawangunk Mountain in New York southwest to Mount Oglethorpe in Georgia. Hawks and other raptors follow Blue Mountain to warmer latitudes on their migrations south in autumn.

Like other ridges, Blue Mountain provides not only a pathway south but also upward-moving air that allows soaring—an energy-saving mode of flight. The birds use two types of rising air currents, thermal and deflective. Thermal air currents are bubbles of air, heated by the sun, which then rise from the earth's surface (in this case the south side of the mountain). Deflective air currents are produced when wind striking a mountainside is forced upward, creating a strong draft.

The hawks do not drift through the air like a dandelion seed, or float on the wind as a piece of grass floats on a current of water. The birds fly through the air using their speed to support themselves. This speed can be the result of wing action, or of the bird's use of gravity. By moving downward at the same rate or more slowly than the rate of air moving upward around it, the bird soars.

0.0 (0.0) *Leaving the entrance to Trexlertown Velodrome, turn right onto Mosser Road.*

The TREXLERTOWN VELODROME, a Lehigh County facility, is a bicycle racing track where cyclists from across the country and around the world compete. Races are held from early May to late October on Tuesday and Friday evenings.

1.4 (1.4) *Junction with Twin Ponds Road; turn right.*

A gentle climb to slate hills brings views of limestone valley farmland—a mosaic of pastures, fields, and woods.

3.5 (2.1) *Intersection with Wood Lane; turn right.*

Hex signs—rural German folk art—are visible on barns in this area, as they are at other points along the tour. The star, lily, or tulip

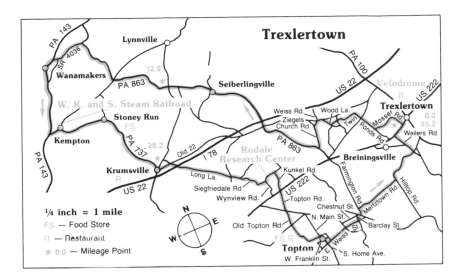

designs, painted in bright colors within a circle, are said to ward off evil. Most experts think the hex sign is merely decorative.

4.2 (0.7) *Intersection with Weiss Road; turn left.*

4.4 (0.2) *Junction with Ziegels Church Road; turn left.*

5.4 (1.0) *Junction with PA 863; turn right.*
PA 863 follows along the hilltops of an area that differs from the flatter southern part of the Great Valley because it is underlain with shale instead of limestone.
  6.2 A tumbledown stone iron furnace, a remnant of nineteenth-century Pennsylvania industry, can be seen on the right roadside.
  10.7 Ahead is BLUE MOUNTAIN, the first ridge of the Ridge and Valley Region, above the rolling shaley hills.
  10.9 Seiberlingsville consists of a few frame buildings on a hill.
  12.0 On the left in the distance on the end of a Blue Mountain prong is THE PINNACLE, an outcrop of white quartzite.

15.4 (10.0) *Intersection with a road to Lynnville; go straight on PA 863.*

17.7 (2.3) *Junction; turn left onto the road to Wanamakers.*
  On the right along the road is Ontelaunee Creek, flowing through farmland.

19.0 (1.3) *"Y" at a bridge; bear right on SR 4037.*

19.2 (0.2) *Junction with PA 143; turn left.*

21.6 Looming above on the right is the Pinnacle, and behind it is HAWK MOUNTAIN, a 2,000-acre private refuge for the protection and study of migrating raptors: hawks, eagles, ospreys, and falcons. The exposed rocks on the mountain were once a favorite position for shooters of the migrating birds. In the 1930s conservationists, alerted to the plight of the raptors, established Hawk Mountain Sanctuary. Now when fall arrives, those sandstone rocks are covered with birdwatchers armed with cameras and binoculars.

22.4 (3.2) *Turn left onto PA 737.*

22.9 Kempton began as a railroad town in 1874. Normal train service ended years ago, but the W.K. AND S. STEAM RAILROAD (215-756-6469) now runs amusement trips on the line along Ontelaunee Creek. The operation is manned by train buff volunteers and runs a steam locomotive passenger train and a trolley. Each trip takes forty minutes.

Near the railroad station is a Pennsylvania barn holding the KEMPTON PENNSYLVANIA DUTCH FARM MUSEUM (May–Oct., 10-6 weekends; charge). The museum contains the farm life collection of a former Pennsylvania Dutch farmer, Howard Geisinger. Mr. Geisinger, who speaks with a strong Dutch accent, takes visitors through the museum himself. Inside are many displays, including cooking utensils, barn-making tools, shoemaker tools, and washing machines.

24.9 Village of Stony Run. Snyders Hotel, now just a bar, is a brick-and-stone structure dating to 1858.

25.8 The Kunkel Gristmill, built in 1838, is the small stone building surrounded by a modern milling operation on the left.

28.2 (5.8) *Intersection with Old 22 in Krumsville; turn left.*

28.7 (0.5) *Intersection with Long Lane; turn right.*
This quiet lane offers views of the surrounding countryside.

30.9 The large stone building on the right is the former Golden Eagle Inn, a structure built before 1816.

31.2 (2.5) *Intersection; go straight onto Siegfriedale Road.*

31.7 (0.5) *"Y"; bear right on Siegfriedale Road.*

32.8 (1.1) *Junction with Wynview Road; turn left.*

33.0 This old farm is the RODALE RESEARCH CENTER (open daily), a scientific experiment station owned by Rodale Press, publishers of *Organic Gardening, Prevention, Bicycling,* and other health and environment-related publications. The center tests organic and low-energy agriculture techniques including backyard fish ponds, solar greenhouses, biological pest control, and new crops. One of the promising new crops is amaranth, a staple of the ancient Aztecs and Incas, which could help ease third world malnutrition. A self-guided tour of the center begins at an old schoolhouse farther up the road.

33.5 (0.7) *Turn right onto Kunkel Road.*

34.3 (0.8) *Intersection with US 222; go straight onto Topton Road.*

Now that it has returned to the limestone part of Great Valley, the route passes fertile fields and large farmsteads. Silos and metal windmills rise above the gently rolling terrain.

36.1 (0.0) *Intersection, go straight onto Old Topton Road.*

37.4 (2.3) *Intersection with North Main Street; turn right.*

37.5 (0.1) *Junction with West Franklin Street in Topton; turn left, then at the intersection with South Home Avenue turn right.*

TOPTON got its name because it is the highest point on the East Penn Railroad between Allentown and Reading. The Kutztown Railroad joins the East Penn here; the town grew in the late 1800s

Rodale Press experimental farm.

as a railroad center. There are a number of old brick factories near the tracks, and Victorian-style buildings dominate the town. The Topton Hotel, now a bar, is a three-story Italianate structure.

37.7 (0.2) *Intersection with East Weiss Street; turn left.*

39.3 (1.6) *Intersection; turn left onto Barclay Street.*

39.6 (0.3) *Junction with Chestnut Street; turn right, then immediately right again, then after 0.1 mile turn left onto Farmington Road.*

39.9 (0.3) *Turn right onto Mertztown Road.*

41.8 (1.9) *Junction with Hilltop Road; turn left.*

    42.2 The white wooden barn on the left has hex signs on its front.

43.4 (1.6) *Intersection in Weilersville; turn left onto the road to Breiningsville.*

43.8 (0.4) *"Y"; bear right on Weilers Road.*

44.5 (0.7) *Junction with US 222; turn right.*

45.1 (0.6) *Turn left on Mosser Road; then go 0.1 mile to Trexlertown Velodrome.*

Bicycle Shops:
Trexlertown Cycle Sports, Route 222, Trexlertown, (215) 398-9696

12 Lebanon Valley

- **Lebanon County**
- **Start and end at Cornwall Iron Furnace (off PA 419, 2 miles east of PA 72)**
- **29.4 miles; flat to rolling with a few hills**
- **1 day**

For many, the name "Pennsylvania Dutch" brings to mind images of plain dress, plain farming, and horse-drawn buggies. While the old order, or plain people, are certainly the most visible Pennsylvania Germans, they number only 60,000. The bulk of the Pennsylvania Dutch population in southeastern Pennsylvania belongs either to what are called "the church people" or "the fringe people." The church people, who number more than 300,000, are descendents of Lutheran, Reformed, and Moravian settlers. They keep the German dialect, ethnic church ties, and some old-world traditions. Close to a million in number, the fringe people have German surnames and often speak with German accents, but they have forsaken most of the old traditions, either in an effort to conform with modern American ideals or because of their closeness to, or intermarriage with, members of other ethnic groups.

Altogether, the Pennsylvania Dutch dominate Berks, Lancaster, Lebanon, and York Counties and form large minorities in ten other Pennsylvania counties. Today 250,000 Pennsylvanians still speak the dialect, although with each generation the number declines. Perhaps the most lasting part of the culture, evident among all three groups, is Pennsylvania Dutch cooking, promoted heavily by area restaurants and including such famous foods as sauerkraut, scrapple, apple butter, and shoofly pie.

0.0 (0.0) *Leaving the entrance to Cornwall Iron Furnace, turn right, then go straight at a stop sign, then bear right at a "Y" onto Rexmont Road.*

CORNWALL IRON FURNACE (9–5 Tues.–Sat., 12–5 Sun., closed certain holidays, 717-272-9711; charge), a state historic site, began operating in 1742, using ore from nearby banks, charcoal from the wooded hills, and limestone from the Great Valley. Cornwall was one of the furnaces that provided cannons, munitions, and equipment for the Continental Army. Iron was produced here until 1883.

The site's red sandstone Gothic buildings were constructed in the 1850s with slit windows, pointed-arch doorways, and butresses.

The buildings now hold museum exhibits explaining the general operation and some restored parts of the furnace.

The nearby iron banks were formed by iron-laden molten rock that spread into layers of limestone bedrock hundreds of millions of years ago. The mine was worked from 1742 to 1973 and is the oldest continuously operated mine in the U.S.

Rexmont Road follows a contour along the slopes of Furnace Hills. Occasionally the woods on the left are broken by views of broad farmland in the Great Valley. Later the route descends to the rich valley floor.

2.9 On the right is HORST'S MILL, a three-and-a-half-story limestone building. Like much of the old architecture in this area, this building has contrasting cornerstones of red sandstone.

3.5 (3.5) *Intersection with Schaeffer Road (PA 419); turn right.*

4.5 (1.0) *Buffalo Springs; turn right onto Distillery Road.*

Here are a number of picturesque limestone barns with red sandstone cornerstones. Slits on the ends allow ventilation.

5.9 (1.4) *Intersection with Michter Road; turn left.*

To the right a short distance is MICHTER'S DISTILLERY (10-5 Mon.–Sat., 12-5 Sun.; charge for tour), an accumulation of brick and frame buildings surrounded by farmland. An immense whiskey jug sits safely atop a brick and glass tower. A distillery has operated at the site since 1753, when John Shenk, a Swiss Mennonite farmer, made whiskey from excess grain. Michter's Distillery claims that George Washington "probably" bought whiskey for his troops here and calls its product "the whiskey that warmed the Revolution." The site is a National Historic Landmark and includes the Distillery Building of a nineteenth-century owner where a small still is demonstrated.

6.7 (0.8) *Intersection with PA 501; go straight onto Market Street.*

7.2 (0.5) *"Y"; bear right onto Market Street.*

7.7 (0.5) *Fountain Park in Schaefferstown; turn right onto Sheep Hill Road.*

Fountain Park was a gift of Alexander Schaeffer to SCHAEFFERSTOWN, the town he laid out in 1744. Schaeffer used the park's spring to feed the water system he developed for the community, one of the first gravitational systems developed in the colonies.

Straight ahead on Market Street is the center of Schaefferstown. Along this street, in the fashion of the old country, are three of the fountains which Schaeffer planned for the town. He also included a market square. Here, too, is the Franklin House, which Schaeffer built as a hotel in the mid-1700s. It is still used as a bar.

THE ALEXANDER SCHAEFFER FARM MUSEUM (by appointment, 717-949-3795), Schaeffer's homestead on the edge of town, is an open-air folk-life museum. The restored stone, one-story farmhouse is a fine example of a traditional Swiss bank house, a European style rare in Pennsylvania. Nearby is a common Pennsylvania, or Swiss bank, barn.

The Schaeffer farmstead is the site of a Folk Festival, held the second weekend in July, with demonstrations of eighteenth-century crafts, preparations of Pennsylvania Dutch foods, and farming exhibitions. The annual Harvest Fair, oriented to farm activities, occurs on the second weekend of September, with the use of horses a major part of the demonstrations and contests.

9.0 (1.3) *"Y"; bear left onto Canaan Grove Road.*

The road becomes rolling and the roadside is mostly wooded with some farms.

10.6 (1.6) *Junction with Hopeland Road; turn left.*

Right here 1.9 miles is the MIDDLE CREEK WILDLIFE MAN-AGEMENT AREA, a wetland managed by the Pennsylvania Game Commission. The area abounds with birds; a large flock of Canada geese is in residence year-round. The VISITORS CENTER (Mar.–Nov. 9–5 Tues.–Sat., 12–5 Sun.; free) has wildlife management displays. Pleasant picnic areas border the wetlands.

10.8 (0.2) *Junction with PA 897; turn right.*

10.9 (0.1) *Kleinfeltersville; turn left onto Millbach Road.*

This pretty tree-shaded hamlet holds the graveyard where Jacob Albright, founder of the Evangelical church, is buried.

13.1 On the right is the HOUSE OF MILLER AT MILLBACH (private), listed on the National Register of Historic Places. Built in 1752, it is a two-and-a-half-story structure made of cut limestone with red sandstone making corners and the arches over the first floor windows and doors. Its Germanic design includes a gambrel roof. Attached is the 1784 mill house.

13.3 (2.4) *Junction with PA 419 in Millbach; turn left, then immediately right onto the road to Richland.*

14.2 The remnants of a stone iron furnace are in a field on the right.

A typical Pennsylvania barn in Schaefferstown.

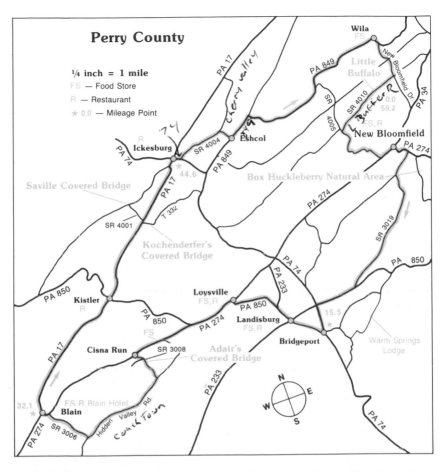

0.0 (0.0) *Leaving the entrance to the swimming and picnicking area at Little Buffalo State Park, turn left onto SR 4010.*

LITTLE BUFFALO STATE PARK, surrounding a manmade lake, is a modern day-use park with picnic areas and a swimming pool. Also in the park is SHOAFF'S MILL, an overshot gristmill which the park service has renovated. In the same area is a covered bridge which was moved from another location.

Nearby is the BLUE BALL TAVERN (June–Aug., 2–4 Sun.), a late-1700s tavern now housing a museum. Blue Ball was the name of several early taverns, and it has become the name of several Pennsylvania communities. It probably originates from the metal ball which once was used to signal stage coaches. A ball propped high meant there was no need to stop—the source of the expression "highballin' it."

1.8 (1.8) *Junction with SR 4005; turn left.*

   2.8 CLARK'S MILL, a three-story stone structure, was built in 1831. Milling operations ceased in 1916.

3.0 (1.2) *"Y"; bear left on SR 4005.*

The restored mill in Little Buffalo State Park.

4.5 (1.5) *Junction with PA 274; turn left.*

5.2 (0.7) *Intersection in New Bloomfield; turn right onto PA 274.*
NEW BLOOMFIELD, a small town with shaded streets, was laid out in 1823 and became Perry County's seat of government in 1827. The county takes pride in its rural character, claiming in one tourist brochure that it does not have a single parking meter or traffic light.

Like many Pennsylvania towns, New Bloomfield has a market square. In its center is a Civil War soldiers-sailors monument, built in 1898. On a corner is the courthouse, a two-story brick structure, built in 1826–27 and topped by an ornate clock and bell tower.

Several blocks from the town square on West Main Street is a little green area that holds the Big Spring. The spring strikes the surface in a circular stone-walled basin, then runs into a small pond inhabited by ducks. Large springs, the surfacing of underground streams, are common in limestone areas.

6.0 (0.8) *Turn right onto SR 3019.*
Straight here 0.2 mile, then right on Huckleberry Road 0.4 mile is the BOX HUCKLEBERRY NATURAL AREA. In 1845 the box huckleberry plant was discovered here. Covering nine acres, it is estimated to be at least 1,300 years old. The plant forms a dark green mat only a few inches high, blossoms in May and June with white or pink flowers, and bears a light blue berry in late summer. The area has a nature trail, which is described in a brochure available at the trailhead.

7.1 (1.1) *"Y"; bear left on SR 3019.*
The route passes through a hillier and more wooded area, the topographic result of erosion-resistant sandstone and siltstone bedrock. Rough terrain and poor soils limit farming here.

12.6 (5.5) *Junction with PA 850; turn right.*
To the right of PA 850 is more of the rough wooded sandstone area. The land to the left, however, is underlain with limestone and shale and is therefore flatter and better for farming. In the distance is Blue Mountain, a high ridge made of quartzite, a ridge-building rock in Pennsylvania.

14.3 (1.7) *Intersection with PA 74 in Alinda; turn left.*

15.5 (1.2) *Intersection in Bridgeport; turn right onto the road to Landisburg (SR 3017).*
Left here 1.4 miles, then left on gravel Warm Springs Road 1.6 miles is Warm Springs Lodge (717-789-9927), an old two-story inn facing Shermans Creek. The warm springs (66°F) inspired the establishment of a health spa here in 1830, and "the waters were

taken" until the turn of the century. Water from the springs was purported to be good as a purgative, powerful as a diuretic, helpful for rheumatism, kidney and liver complaints, dyspepsia, gout, Bright's disease (diabetes), eczema, sore eyes, and general weaknesses of constitution. The present owners do not make all these claims; they simply offer comfortable lodging and tasty meals.

Straight ahead 0.2 mile is the H.R. WENTZEL AND SONS MILL. This stone building was constructed in 1805. The mill still operates, producing Ivory brand flour and cornmeal.

17.0 (1.5) *Intersection in Landisburg; go straight onto PA 850.*

The village of LANDISBURG was laid out by Abraham Landis in 1793. It served as the county seat when Perry County was formed in 1820, and before the seat was moved to New Bloomfield in 1827.

21.4 On the right is WAGGONER'S COVERED BRIDGE, a red painted bridge built in 1889.

21.9 (4.9) *Turn left onto PA 274.*

24.5 (2.6) *Cisna Run; turn left onto SR 3008.*

24.9 The route crosses ADAIR'S COVERED BRIDGE, which spans Shermans Creek. It was built in 1864 using Burr truss construction, a design using curved beams on the interior bridge sides.

25.0 TROSTLE MILL, a tall brick structure, once operated with a water turbine.

25.9 (1.4) *Junction with Hidden Valley Road; turn right.*

29.9 (4.0) *Turn right onto SR 3006.*

31.6 SMITH MILL, a wooden structure on the right, was built by James Blaine in 1778. Today it operates under electric power as a feed mill.

31.8 (1.9) *Junction with PA 274 in Loysville; turn left.*

32.1 (0.3) *Blain; go straight onto PA 17.*

BLAIN, a village of white frame houses, is surrounded by cornfields in the middle of a valley. It grew around the mill that James Blaine built in 1778. At one time it was known as Multicaulisville after *Moros Multicaulis*, or the Italian mulberry, which a leading citizen was culturing for silkworms. The simpler "Blain" was chosen in 1846. Blain's big event is its annual Blain Picnic at the town's picnic grounds, held in mid-August, and offering arts, home cooking, and antique machinery demonstrations.

The Blain Hotel (717-536-3322) is a plain country hotel, operated like a tourist home with the owner's family occupying part of the building. An unusual feature of the hotel is a solar heating system which the owner is glad to explain. A diner-like restaurant operates on the first floor.

From Blain, PA 17, a quiet highway, passes through prosperous farmland in a limestone valley. On the left looms Tuscarora Mountain, a quartzite ridge. Sandstone forms a broken ridge along the right.

41.6 T 332 joins on the right, then SR 4001 joins on the left.
Right here 0.2 mile is KOCHENDERFER'S COVERED BRIDGE, built in 1919 over Big Buffalo Creek. Left here on SR 4001 0.9 mile is the hamlet of Saville, where the SAVILLE COVERED BRIDGE spans Big Buffalo Creek.

44.6 (12.5) *Intersection with PA 74 in Ickesburg; turn right.*
Ickesburg is another pleasant village.

44.9 (0.3) *Turn left onto SR 4004.*

46.9 (2.0) *"Y"; bear right on SR 4004.*
The route passes through a gap in the low sandstone ridge which has paralleled the route since the intersection with PA 850 in Kistler.

47.5 (0.6) *Intersection with PA 849 in Eshcol; turn left.*
PA 849 follows Big Buffalo Creek through a partially wooded valley. The land consists of soil based on underlying shale and is relatively unfertile, compared to the limestone soil of the PA 17 valley. Farms here are small and homes are often in disrepair. Along the route are several small communities.

56.1 (8.6) *"Y" after Wila; bear right onto New Bloomfield Drive.*
The route crosses a low sandstone ridge, then drops to Little Buffalo Creek.

57.9 (1.8) *Intersection with SR 4010; turn right.*

59.2 (1.3) *Little Buffalo State Park.*

Bicycle Shop:
Delancey Bicycle and Machine Shop, 232 West Main, New Bloomfield, (717) 582-2028

15 Kishacoquillas Valley

- **Mifflin County**
- **Start and end at Reeds Gap State Park**
- **55.2 miles; flat to rolling with a few hills**
- **1 or 2 days**

Kishacoquillas Valley (or Big Valley), with its broad fertile limestone floor, attracted Amish farmers as early as 1791. Only a small number of families settled here (among them the Zooks, Yoders, Peachys, and Speichers) and at first they all belonged to one church. But the years have brought divisions in belief among these families, so that today Big Valley has more religious groups than any other Amish-Mennonite area in North America.

The groups rank themselves from "low" to "high" church. A low church is one that has retained the old traditions, while a high church is one that is more modern. Besides variations in their willingness to use present-day technology, the separate groups can be distinguished by their buggy styles, their dress, and by the appearance of their homes. The differences in buggy top color has led, in fact, to a local nomenclature for the Amish divisions:

The "white tops" or "Old School" Amish are the most traditional of all Amish in North America. The men have shoulder-length hair and wear white shirts, brown denim trousers, wide-brimmed hats, no suspenders, and no belts. Women wear long dark dresses and dark kerchiefs over white coverings on their heads. The old schoolers do not paint their barns, and they rarely paint their houses. Curtains and window screens are taboo. Small engines can be used, but only for belt power.

The "yellow top" group or the "Byler Church" is also known as the "Beansoupers" after their practice of serving bean soup for lunch following the preaching service. Men's hair falls over the ears, and colored shirts—typically blue—are allowed. Women wear brown bonnets. All buildings are painted, and half-length curtains, blinds, and screens are used.

The "black top" Amish or "Renno Amish" is a higher church. Men wear a single suspender and their hair covers their ears. Women wear dark plain-colored dresses, black bonnets, white starched head coverings, and black shawls. Barns are usually red, houses white, and window blinds and half-length curtains are common.

Several other higher Amish churches, more open to modern

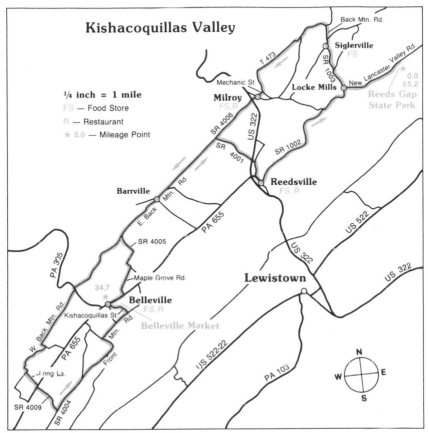

Kishacoquillas Valley

¼ inch = 1 mile
FS — Food Store
R — Restaurant
★ 0.0 — Mileage Point

conveniences, exist in Big Valley. The "Beachy Church" or "Speicher" group allows tractors, automobiles, electricity, and kitchen appliances. Other groups have splintered off and joined Mennonite conferences. Lower church groups among these emphasize plain clothing but allow automobiles and electricity. Higher Mennonite church groups are practically indistinguishable from modern society.

0.0 (0.0) *Leaving the entrance to Reeds Gap State Park, turn left onto New Lancaster Valley Road.*

REEDS GAP STATE PARK offers picnicking, pool swimming (with showers), and tent camping in a pleasant hemlock grove along a small stream. In the late eighteenth century the site was a meeting ground where local families gathered to hear circuit preachers. In the nineteenth century a sawmill operated here. A recreation area was established under the C.C.C. program.

From Reeds Gap the route passes through wooded New Lancaster Valley as it widens to join Big Valley.

2.7 (2.7) *Junction; turn right onto the road to Siglerville.*

On the left Jacks Mountain continues into the distance, forming the southern border of Kishacoquillas Valley. The route skirts the steep-forested end of Thick Mountain's ridge line on the right. Later, views appear to the right of Strong Mountain's end rising above the valley farmland, and beyond it Long Mountain, a ridge that borders the north part of Big Valley. All four ridges are capped with Tuscarora quartzite, a tough rock whose resistance has prevented erosion from carrying these mountains away.

3.7 (1.0) *"Y"; bear left onto SR 1003 (main road).*

4.8 (1.1) *Junction in Siglerville; turn right onto Back Mountain Road.*

Siglerville, a village of simple Georgian homes on Havice Creek, was settled in 1847 by Joseph Sigler who built a blacksmith shop there. The town's general store is in its old schoolhouse.

7.0 (2.2) *"Y"; bear right onto T 473 (unmarked).*

In the distance across this slightly rolling farmland is the beginning of Sand Hole Ridge, which continues down the valley.

10.3 (3.3) *Turn right onto Mechanic Street.*

10.6 (0.3) *Junction in Milroy; turn right, then immediately left onto SR 4006.*

Milroy is a small town of Georgian-style frame houses and a winding main street. U.S. 322 passes on one side.

10.8 (0.2) *Junction with US 322; turn right, then immediately left on SR 4006.*

12.0 An Amish sawmill is on the right.

13.3 An Amish one-room schoolhouse is on the left.

13.6 The Amish farmstead on the left, belonging to a "white top" farmer, includes two houses, parts of which have been left unpainted. There are no curtains in the windows.

16.0 The Amish farmhouse on the left is two houses end-to-end. One is the "grandfather house" where the retired parents stay. Besides having a separate living unit, grandparents keep their own horse and buggy.

16.3 (5.5) *"Y" in Barrville; bear left onto East Back Mountain Road (unmarked).*

Stone Mountain, the wooded ridge paralleling the route on the right, has a shelf about midway up, a layer of resistant sandstone. The top of the ridge is Tuscarora quartzite.

18.6 (2.3) *Where SR 4005 turns left, go straight onto East Back Mountain Road.*

19.1 The depression by a clump of trees in the field on the right is a sinkhole, a common feature of limestone valleys, created when surface dirt and gravel falls into a cave.

19.9 Gray one-room school ahead.

20.3 Another sinkhole is on the left, in front of a farmstead.

21.3 A white cinderblock one-room schoolhouse is on the left. Amish schoolhouses are located within walking distance of every child's home.

The fancier homes with curtains and larger farms through this area belong to "black top" Amish.

21.5 (2.9) *Junction with PA 305; turn left, then after 0.1 mile turn right onto West Back Mountain Road.*

Peachy is a prominent name on mail boxes and businesses in this section.

As the route climbs slightly, several views appear of the eastern end of Kishacoquillas Valley, a fertile farmland dotted with silos and hemmed by blue ridges.

24.6 (3.1) *Right onto Back Mountain Road.*

26.2 (1.6) *Immediately after the road turns sharply right, turn left onto Long Lane.*

To the right at several points are views of the west end of Kishacoquillas Valley, which narrows as the bordering ridges come together.

26.9 (0.7) *Junction with PA 655; turn right, then immediately left onto SR 4009.*

28.3 (1.4) *Junction with SR 4004; turn left.*

29.9 (1.6) *"Y"; bear right onto Front Mountain Road.*

Climbing steeply to the right, Jacks Mountain continues down the valley. Flat limestone farmland with broad fields and large farms lies to the left.

32.3 (2.4) *Turn right on Front Mountain Road.*

32.8 The one-story brick building on the left is the Belleville Mennonite School.

33.8 (1.5) *Left onto Kishacoquillas Street.*

Straight ahead 0.3 mile, then right on a lane 0.2 mile, is Peight's

Store, a general store serving the area's Amish and Mennonites. The building is filled with interesting food, clothing, and other items.

34.4 On the right is the entrance to the BELLEVILLE MARKET grounds. Not long after sunrise on Wednesday mornings, the place starts buzzing with arriving Amish wagons loaded with hogs, chickens, and other livestock, women with pies and preserves setting up their stands, and flea market dealers laying out an assortment of junk.

Before long the crowds arrive—Amish women with baskets, tourists from the city, young housewives with children—to file past the rows of flea market tables and produce stands or to visit the produce auction barn. By mid-day the women and tourists are mostly gone, the flea market closes up, and the men gather in a rustic auditorium for the livestock auction. Here, Amishmen in broad-brimmed hats discuss the merits of passing livestock, old lard cans catch tobacco salivations, and the auctioneer's chant is the afternoon's entertainment.

34.7 (0.9) *Junction with PA 355 in Belleville; turn right.*

BELLEVILLE, a busy town with scattered businesses, is the main commercial center of the valley. Its importance to the local Amish can be guessed from the various shops selling gas refrigerators and Coleman lanterns.

35.4 (0.7) *Turn left onto Maple Grove Road.*

35.6 The Maple Grove Mennonite Church is on the left. Maple Grove Mennonites comprise the highest church of the Amish-related groups in Big Valley. They drive cars, use electricity, and dress as they please, but they still consider their church "lower" than the general Protestant churches in the area.

The route travels across the middle of this wide valley through fields and pastures, past neat homes with healthy gardens. Yoder is a common name on mailboxes.

38.1 (2.7) *"Y"; bear right onto the road to Barrville.*

The Amish farmhouses along this road are typically white or unpainted. Large gardens are nearby, sometimes surrounded by picket fences, and ducks, geese, and chickens run freely around the yards. Each farmstead has a small orchard. Various pieces of farm machinery, some motorized, sit outside the barns.

41.0 (2.9) *"Y"; bear left onto East Back Mountain Road (unmarked).*

Near many driveways along this road are stands holding Amish milk cans waiting to be picked up.

43.9 (2.9) *Turn right onto the road to Reedsville.*

The route follows a mostly wooded ravine past several non-Amish farms.

45.8 (1.9) *Junction; turn right onto the road to Reedsville.*

46.5 (0.7) *Junction with PA 655; turn left.*

46.8 (0.3) *Stoplight in Reedsville; turn left on SR 1002.*

REEDSVILLE, a small town at a water gap in Jacks Mountain, was settled around 1750 and laid out in 1838. The old Black Horse Tavern there has a bar entrance and a lounge entrance, as English pubs do. A small park is situated where Honey Creek flows along the edge of town.

51.1 (4.3) *Junction; turn right onto the road to Locke Mills.*

52.6 (1.5) *Turn right onto New Lancaster Valley Road.*

55.2 (2.6) *Reeds Gap State Park.*

Bicycle Shops:
None on route. The nearest shop is in Lewistown.

16 Central Pennsylvania

- **Centre and Clinton Counties**
- **Start and end at State College**
- **79.4 miles; flat to rolling with a few climbs**
- **1 or 2 days, overnight stop at Woodward Cave (mile 33.7) or Millheim Hotel (mile 34.5)**

Local iron industries made the town of Bellefonte thrive during the nineteenth century. Prosperity brought prominence: five of Pennsylvania's governors came from Bellefonte, and two former residents became governors of other states. The town vibrated with the new ideas of writers, poets, and inventors. Thomas Edison chose Bellefonte as his second site for community electrical illumination.

Bellefonte showed off its prosperity and prominence with buildings of the day's most stylish and expensive architecture. The town's residential streets were tree-shaded and lined with substantial houses; its business section held a Greek Revival courthouse and two magnificent hotels. Bellefontonians had good reason to be proud of their town.

But then it all changed. Minnesota's Mesabi iron was discovered in 1844, and the opening of the Sault Ste. Marie locks in 1855 allowed Great Lakes shipping of that iron. The Bessemer steel-making process was perfected by 1856. The final blow was the formation of U.S. Steel at the end of the century. Bellefonte simply could not compete.

To make matters worse, Bellefonte's upstart young neighbor, State College, boomed when World War II veterans took their G.I. Bill benefits to Pennsylvania State College (soon renamed the Pennsylvania State University). Bellefonte's businesses began migrating to State College. So did the county's daily newspaper and the telephone company office. Even the mayor of Bellefonte quit his position in order to live in State College. Bellefontonians began remarking sourly that "State College'll steal the courthouse next if we don't watch out."

0.0 (0.0) *Leaving front drive of Hetzel Union Building, Pennsylvania State University, turn right onto Pollock Road.*

PENNSYLVANIA STATE UNIVERSITY was founded in 1855 as the Farmers' High School, and for a number of years it consisted of one four-story Gothic Revival building set in the middle of a pasture. Its first class of sixty-nine students was taught by four professors. Today classroom buildings, office buildings, and resi-

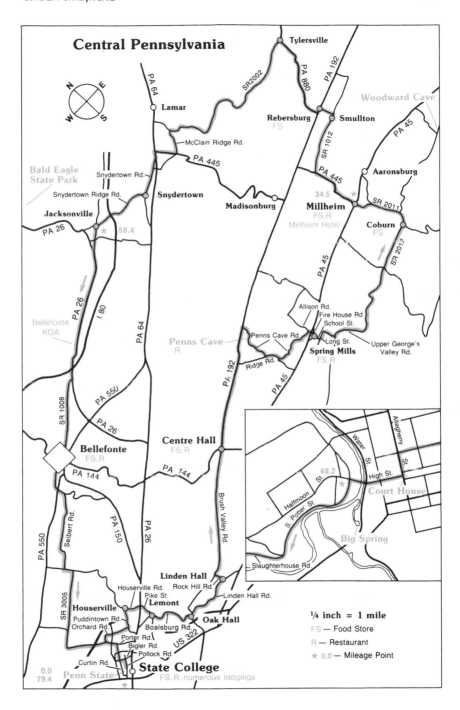

Central Pennsylvania

FS — Food Store
R — Restaurant
★ 0.0 — Mileage Point

¼ inch = 1 mile

dence halls cover a campus of 540 acres. Enrollment is approximately 33,500, with a faculty of nearly 1,900 at the main campus. Twenty-two branch campuses are scattered about the state.

The beauty of the University Park campus can be partly attributed to interesting and attractive architecture such as columned Old Main or Georgian West Halls. Well-landscaped grounds add to the charm, especially the numerous flower beds and the walkways lined with elms. The university also boasts several fine museums associated with various departments. The unusual Earth and Mineral Science Museum features an array of beautiful gems and minerals and many exhibits on mineral industries.

STATE COLLEGE adjoins and serves the campus. It is a young town, both in its own age and in the ages of its inhabitants. Photos taken as late as 1910 show sows wallowing in a muddy street that now is one of the town's main avenues. Recently State College became a Standard Metropolitan Statistical Area, a major urban area under the classification scheme of the U.S. Census Bureau. It is one of the larger college towns in the nation and its youthful populace attracts an assortment of electronic arcades, a wide selection of specialty restaurants, and a multitude of movie houses. The young ideals of the community along with continuous prosperity have maintained high esthetic standards, making the town a nice place both to visit and to live in.

0.3 (0.3) *Intersection with Bigler Road; turn left, then at the next intersection turn right onto Curtin Road.*

0.9 Like an old grey battleship, BEAVER STADIUM sits on a sea of rolling hills in what Penn State students call Happy Valley. On brisk fall days the grounds around the stadium fill with automobiles as fans of the Nittany Lions arrive from all parts of the state and beyond.

1.1 (0.8) *Junction with Porter Road; turn left.*

1.6 (0.5) *"Y"; bear right onto Orchard Road (unmarked).*

3.1 (1.5) *Junction with Puddintown Road; turn left.*

3.9 (0.8) *Junction with Houserville Road in Houserville; turn right.*

4.7 (0.8) *Intersection with East College Avenue; go straight onto Pike Street.*

5.3 (0.6) *Intersection in Lemont; turn left onto Boalsburg Road.*

Unlike many of the old, small towns in Nittany Valley, LEMONT continued to grow and prosper after it lost its importance as a crossroads agricultural community. Today it is a bedroom community for professors and university employees.

6.6 After traveling around the abrupt end of Nittany Mountain on the left, the route passes a limestone quarry where the ridge's rock layers can be seen pointing upward towards the middle of Penns Valley. Many millions of years ago, after this rock formed from accumulated sediments, a collision of continents squeezed the earth's crust, building the Appalachian Mountains. Here were deformed previously flat-lying layers, like the layers of a newspaper pushed against a wall. Originally, Nittany Mountain was beneath the trough of a fold, while Nittany and Penns Valleys on its sides were under a crest; in other words, the topography was reversed from what it is today.

For a long time after this collision the forces of nature wore away at the wrinkled terrain, working longer on harder rock and higher elevations, and eventually making a nearly flat plain. Geologic forces then raised the plain, and erosion began again to cut the land down to base level. This process may have been repeated several times.

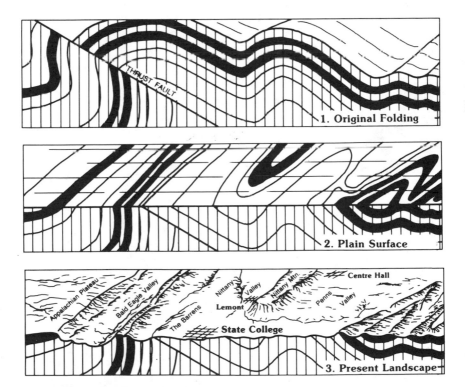

The land is now being worn down again. Since Nittany Mountain is capped by a trowel-shaped layer of hard sandstone, it has resisted erosion. But that protective layer—once arching over the valleys—was lopped off during the last wearing down, exposing weak limestone which easily wore away.

7.4 (2.1) *Turn left across a bridge, then go straight onto Linden Hall Road.*

9.6 (2.2) *Stop sign in Linden Hall; turn left onto Rock Hill Road; then at a bend bear right onto Brush Valley Road.*
LINDEN HALL is a hamlet of scattered homes around a small pond. The "Hall" suffix, common among town names in this area, reflects early settlement by Anglo-Saxon farmers. It is an imitation of the English "hall," used to refer to a manor house with an adjacent village.

12.4 The house and barn on the left are representative of the architectural styles that settlers brought to this valley from southeastern Pennsylvania. The barn is a Pennsylvania adaptation of the Swiss barn whose distinctive overhang, called a forebay, shelters barnyard animals. The house is a mixture of German and English architectural features, a souvenir of the period before the English Georgian house style was completely accepted by Pennsylvania Germans. Its exterior, in essence, is Georgian—symmetrical, with chimneys on the outer walls. However, the double front doors indicate a German three-room first floor, with the kitchen the largest and most important room.

15.2 (5.6) *Junction with PA 144 in Centre Hall; go straight onto PA 192.*
CENTRE HALL, named for its position in the center of Penns Valley, still serves as an agricultural market center, with a bank, grocery store, drug store, livestock barn, and several other small businesses. Vestiges remain of a time when transportation was slower and Centre Hall served more functions. The widening in the main street at the center of town was the "diamond" where farmers and craftsmen sold their goods on market day. A large apartment building on the diamond was once a hotel. Near the edge of the business district, a railroad station stands on an abandoned right of way.
Another reminder of Centre Hall's agricultural heritage—but this one a feature whose importance has not diminished—is the Centre County Grange Fair. Held each year during the last week of August, the fair draws some 8,000 week-long residents, many of whom occupy identical green canvas tents which are set up row

upon row. The fair began in 1874 as a day-long picnic, designed to offer farmers some relief from the isolation and monotony of rural life. Today it fulfills the same purpose, with the addition of thrilling amusement rides, top-name country-and-western entertainment, and numerous concessions (serving such delectables as funnel cake and hot sausage).

20.2 (5.0) *Right onto Penns Cave Road.*

Few who have traveled the byways of Pennsylvania have missed the "Visit Penns Cave" billboard. PENNS CAVE (Feb. 15-Nov. 30, 814-364-1664; charge) is "America's Only All Water Cavern." Visitors are ferried through an underground waterway, past numerous fascinating formations, the work of dripping water over countless ages. Well-practiced guides recite an explanation of the cave's origin (sprinkled with expressions such as "nature's flawless beauty"), note the names of formations (everyone is expected to see resemblances to a Chinese dragon and the Statue of Liberty), and recall legends surrounding the cave (like the one about French trapper Melachi Boyer who eloped with Indian Princess Nitanee but was caught by angry Indian relatives and thrown into the cave to die). One wonders if cave guides were on hand to assist in Boyer's torture.

Caves are common in the limestone valleys of Pennsylvania. Limestone is a layer of bedrock formed from the shells of pre-historic sea life. Where erosion has exposed it, particularly good soil results—hence the prosperous farms in these valleys. In addition, strange holes in the ground appear, some considered nuisances, others considered business opportunities. Penn's Cave is the result of limestone's dissolving away along bedrock cracks, creating voids directly by solution or by the collapse of limestone blocks. The stalagmites, stalactites and other popular cave formations are hardened deposits of formerly dissolved limestone, resulting from slow dripping and flowing of water over long periods of time.

21.9 (1.7) *Junction with Ridge Road; turn left.*

22.5 (0.6) *Where a bridge joins on the right, go straight on Penns Cave Road.*

24.4 (1.9) *Junction with Allison Road; turn right, cross PA 45, then turn right at the junction with Fire House Road.*

24.6 (0.2) *Spring Mills; turn left onto School Street, then turn left at the junction with Long Street.*

SPRING MILLS, a village of frame houses in the shadow of Egg

Hill, was named for Rising Spring, found opposite the Spring Mills Hotel. Large springs (this one has a median flow of 6,000 gallons per minute) are also common features of limestone areas. They are often the resurgence of surface streams that have been diverted to underground routes.

25.7 (1.1) *Junction with Upper George's Valley Road; turn left.*

30.0 (4.3) *Intersection; go straight on SR 2012.*

32.0 (2.0) *Junction in Coburn; turn left.*
    COBURN is a village located on Penns Creek where the stream enters the rugged Seven Mountains region through a spectacular gap. Scattered about in the vicinity of Coburn is a community of people, most of them middle-aged, locally known as the Penns Valley Hippies. Many were once associated in some way with Penn State University and with the peace movement during the 60s. Soon after that tumultuous period they rejected the popular definitions of success, and now they enjoy unhurried lifestyles as farmers and craftsmen in this beautiful valley. One couple, for example, lives on a farmstead they built themselves. Their cottage is furnished with electricity from a windmill, lighting from propane and kerosene lanterns, and heat from a wood stove. The small acreage surrounding their home is tilled by work horses, and a garden provides much of their food.

33.7 (1.7) *"Y" after bridge; bear left onto SR 2011.*
        The right fork continues on along Pine Creek 4.2 miles to WOOD
    WARD CAVE (year-round, 814-349-9800; charge), a dry cave
    claimed to be Pennsylvania's largest. This cave has formations with
    remarkable resemblances to everything from a "strip of bacon" to a
    "figure of Christ." A campground and picnic grove are at the site.

34.5 (0.8) *Intersection with PA 45 in Millheim; go straight onto PA 445.*
    MILLHEIM, a small town in eastern Penns Valley, consists of close-spaced Georgian homes near its center, and architecture of later periods with larger yards farther out. The name is roughly German for "home of the mills" and reflects the German population at this crossroads during the early 1800s. Even today German names predominate on business signs and residential mail boxes. Millheim has a public swimming pool.
    The Millheim Hotel (814-349-5994), a quaint structure with a second-story porch that is covered with potted flowers, is one of the small number of Pennsylvania stage-route inns still catering to overnight guests. Its rooms are simply yet comfortably furnished, and the bathroom (with a large iron bathtub) is down the hall. The

hotel also has a dining room with tin ceilings and old photos. It offers both common and vegetarian fare. The bar is a local gathering place.

Right from Millheim on PA 45, 1.0 mile, is AARONSBURG, an attractive village. Settled prior to 1775, it was laid out by Aaron Levy, a Jewish merchant, who hoped the community would become Pennsylvania's capital because of its central position in the state. His plan for a boulevard can still be seen in the wide housing setback on the village's main street. The Aaronsburg Historical Museum (for hours call 814-349-5328) in an old church holds materials dealing with Penns Valley history, including clothing, fancy work, and hand tools.

PA 445 passes through the Millheim Narrows, a steep narrow chasm through Brush Mountain. This watergap was probably created when Elk Creek slowly cut into a fault in the mountain.

36.7 (2.2) *Turn right onto the road to Smullton (SR 1012).*

Straight ahead on PA 445 0.8 mile, then left on PA 192 1.5 miles, is the village of Madisonburg. Over the past several decades Amish have moved to this secluded valley because of scarce land in Lancaster and Mifflin counties. In Madisonburg is the MADISONBURG BAKE SHOP (Thurs., Fri., and Sat.), an Amish bakery selling pastries and sometimes other food such as bean soup and homemade root beer. Madisonburg also has an Amish leather and tack shop.

39.3 (2.6) *After Smullton, turn left over a bridge.*

39.8 (0.5) *Junction with PA 192 in Rebersburg; turn left, then immediately right onto PA 880.*

40.3 On the right and left just before the highway begins climbing Nittany Mountain are several depressions in the valley floor. These are sinkholes, another common feature of limestone areas and the result of the earth's surface falling into a cave.

44.5 (4.7) *Junction in Tylersville; turn left onto SR 2002.*

Sugar Valley's fertile and well-kept farm lands and its remote location in the mountains present an almost Shangri-La atmosphere. The mood is enhanced by a sizeable Amish community which has found this valley to their liking in recent years.

The Lamar road leaves Sugar Valley via the watergap of Fishing Creek. Fishing Creek is a noted trout stream which has attracted both the summer cabins of fishermen and a national fish hatchery. The gap was once proposed as a route for Interstate 80, but it was saved by fishermen and other admirers of the area's beauty.

52.1 (7.6) *Turn left onto McClain Ridge Road.*

53.1 (1.0) *Junction with PA 445; turn right.*

53.9 (0.8) *Junction with PA 64; turn left, then after 0.3 mile turn* *right onto Snydertown Road.*

55.7 (1.8) *Snydertown; turn right onto Snydertown Ridge Road.*
    After Snydertown the route passes over a low, wooded hill known as Sand Ridge. During the building of the Appalachians, the stress at some points was so great that rock layers cracked or faulted. In some cases the bedrock on one side of the fault was pushed up and over the bedrock on the other side. This occurred in Nittany Valley, and Sand Ridge is very old rock that was brought to the surface. Locals call these areas "the barrens" because of the poor sandy soil which barely supports vegetation—and consequently anyone who attempts to farm it.

58.4 (2.7) *Intersection in Jacksonville; turn left.*

58.9 (0.5) *Intersection; go straight onto PA 26.*
        Right on PA 26 3.4 miles, then right on PA 150 1.5 miles, is BALD EAGLE STATE PARK (814-625-2775), with picnicking and swimming at Sayers Lake. The park tent camping area (no showers) is on the south side of the lake near Howard.

64.7 (5.8) *After passing under Interstate 80, turn right onto a*

The Brockerhoff Hotel, one of Bellefonte's many outstanding buildings.

restaurant entrance, then left onto SR 1008.

67.9 (3.2) *Intersection with Allegheny Street in Bellefonte; turn left, then at the courthouse turn right onto High Street.*

BELLEFONTE, a hilly water gap town, was named by Talleyrand, the great French statesman, after the town's Big Spring. The county seat is supposed to have been established at Bellefonte after several town fathers dragged a loaded flatboat up shallow Spring Creek to prove that the town was at the head of navigable water.

Bellefonte is worth a walk through to see its fine old architecture. A historic walking tour map is useful and can be obtained free of charge at the Chamber of Commerce office in the train station. The Centre County Historical Museum (9–5 Mon.–Sat.; free) holds 1,500 items of county historical interest.

68.2 (0.3) *After crossing railroad tracks, turn left onto South Potter Street (unmarked).*

68.6 (0.4) *"Y"; bear left onto Slaughterhouse Road (unmarked).*

69.5 (0.9) *Intersection with PA 550; go straight onto Seibert Road.*

69.8 (0.3) *"Y"; bear right onto Seibert Road.*

73.0 (3.2) *Junction; turn left.*

73.4 (0.4) *Turn right toward the airport onto SR 3005.*

78.6 (5.2) *After Beaver Stadium, turn right onto Curtin Road.*

79.2 (0.6) *Intersection with Bigler Road; turn left, then at the next intersection turn right onto Pollack Road and go to Hetzel Union Building.*

Bicycle Shops:
The Bicycle Shop, 411 West College Avenue, State College, (814) 238-9422
Pedals, 321 East Beaver Avenue, State College, (814) 237-5961
Strada Bicycle Shop, 232-A West College Avenue, State College, (814) 238-0020

17 Buffalo Valley

- **Union County**
- **Start and end at Lewisburg**
- **51.9 miles; flat to rolling with some hills**
- **1 or 2 days; overnight stop at Mifflinburg Hotel (mile 40.3)**

When Sebastian Leininger and his family settled on Penns Creek in what is today Union County, he hoped to find the peace and prosperity that were lacking in his native Germany. Penns Creek was wilderness in the mid-1700s, but other families were clearing land and building cabins. There would be neighbors for the Leiningers and playmates for their two sons and two daughters.

Not long afterward, a battle between the British and French far off on the Ohio River sent Indians on the warpath throughout the Pennsylvania frontier. News of this danger did not reach the Penns Creek pioneers. On one crisp fall day in 1755, Frau Leininger went to the mill with one of her boys. When she returned to the cabin in the evening she found that Indians had killed her husband and other son and had taken off Barbara, twelve, and Regina, ten.

Three years later when Frau Leininger was living in Tulpehocken near Lancaster, she learned that Barbara and another captured girl had escaped from the Indians. It was a joyful reunion, especially when Barbara reported that when she had last seen her, Regina was well. Frau Leininger went on hoping to hear from her second daughter.

On the frigid last day of 1764, more than nine years after the Penns Creek raid, Frau Leininger joined an excited crowd at Carlisle's Market Square. British Colonel Henry Bouquet had defeated the Indians at Bushy Run, and over two hundred captives were free to reunite with relatives. Frau Leininger looked around, but Regina was now eighteen years old, a grown woman, and not the little girl she had last seen. The commissioners asked if there were any way Frau Leininger could attract her daughter's attention with something she would know. Yes, she replied, Regina often used to sing the hymns, "Jesus I Love Evermore," and "Alone, and Yet Not Alone Am I in My Dread Solitude." Hardly had she spoken when Regina sprang from the crowd, recited the Creed and the Lord's Prayer, and sang the hymns.

0.0 (0.0) *Intersection of Water Street and Market Street (PA 45) in Lewisburg; head west on Market Street.*

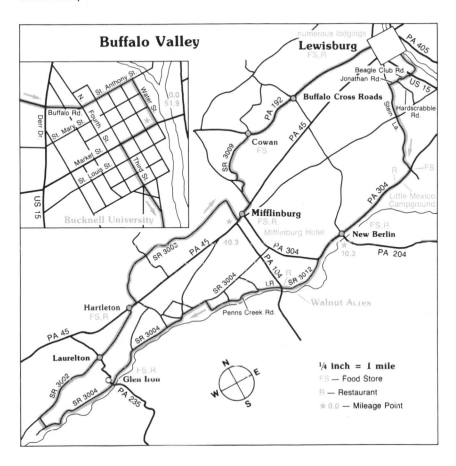

LEWISBURG, a large, attractive town on the Susquehanna River, was laid out in 1785 by Ludwig Derr, the town's first settler. Lewis is the English form of the German "Ludwig." Lewisburg's original German inhabitants left street names beginning with "St."— an early sign painter's abbreviation of *Strasse*, not the abbreviation for "Saint."

Lewisburg's business section, residential streets, and the Bucknell University campus are filled with impressive architecture. After the 1833 construction of a river dam which allowed canal boats to reach the town from the West Branch Canal, new industry and trade caused Lewisburg to blossom. The mostly brick Georgian homes and shops, with their characteristic symmetry and eave-side facing front, can be seen along Market Street from Front Street to Fifth Street.

When Lewisburg became the county seat in 1855, the community experienced an even greater period of growth. Now larger Georgian Revival buildings went up along Market Street from Fifth to Eighth Street. These structures have large windows, and many have porches. Later in this period, Victorian styles appeared—the massive Romanesque, the eclectic Queen Anne, and the strongly vertical Gothic. Also, stylish modifications of older structures occurred, such as the addition of jigsawed gingerbread work. Large bracketed cornices were added to the eaves of Georgian buildings. The drug store at Second and Market Streets, for example, is a log building which was remodeled in the Queen Anne style and has an added conical tower and colored glass windows.

The PACKWOOD MUSEUM (717-524-0323; charge) was built of logs to be a tavern at the end of the 1700s. It now holds exhibits of period furniture and decorative arts. One room is furnished as a turn-of-the-century kitchen. The ELI SLIFER HOME (717-524-2271), one mile north of town on River Road, is a furnished 1860s Tuscan villa mansion, an example of Lewisburg's prosperity at that time.

There are many motels on the outskirts of Lewisburg, but more interesting lodging can be found at the Hotel Lewisburger (717-523-1216) on Market Street. Built in the 1830s as Kline's Hotel, it has been extensively remodeled—including the addition of a Mount Vernon front—over the years. It features a turn-of-the-century oak-paneled dining room.

0.2 (0.2) *Intersection with Third Street; turn left.*

Third Street leaves the business district, first passing through a neighborhood of Georgian row houses, then between Bucknell University on the right and the Susquehanna River on the left. Bucknell is a highly respected private institution with a beautiful, shaded campus.

Georgian architecture in Lewisburg.

2.1 (1.9) *Intersection with US 15; go straight onto Beagle Club Road.*

2.8 (0.7) *Junction with Hardscrabble Road; turn right, then go straight onto Jonathan Road.*

3.2 (0.4) *Junction with Stein Lane (unmarked); turn left.*
Stein Lane passes through a valley floor farming area, then climbs Shamokin Mountain, a low wooded ridge.

7.0 (3.8) *Intersection with PA 304; turn right.*
PA 304 follows agricultural Dry Valley, eventually paralleling Penns Creek.

10.3 (3.3) *Intersection in New Berlin; go straight on PA 304.*
NEW BERLIN, a quiet village of wide maple-shaded streets and Georgian homes, is located on Penns Creek. In 1815 New Berlin, then consisting of log cabins, became the seat of government for newly formed Union County, and over the next forty years the town prospered in that capacity, with more substantial stone, brick, and frame homes replacing log ones. Then in 1855 Union County was divided, and the county seat moved to Lewisburg. New Berlin was left in the backwater and did not change significantly after the mid-1800s. In a way this has been fortunate, for now the village provides a rare opportunity to sense the atmosphere of a sophisticated early-nineteenth-century town.

During its heyday, New Berlin was the fountainhead for the Evangelical Church in America, started by Jacob Albright. The town held the organization's first church, first publishing house, and its first institution of higher learning, Union Seminary. Church tradition has it that the Reverend John Walter, a follower of Albright, arrived in New Berlin one day expecting to preach in a one-room school. The school door was found locked, so he began preaching to a crowd on the school steps. Suddenly the door burst open. Walter led the people into the school and proclaimed that "God has opened us a door in New Berlin and he will establish his work here in spite of the opposition of hell and that of wicked men."

Of interest on the small market square in New Berlin is the Old Courthouse, a brick Georgian structure with a cupola. Nearby, at the corner of Plum and Market, is a limestone residence that was once the sheriff's headquarters and jail—its basement windows still have iron gratings.

On the fourth Saturday in August, the town square is the site of Historic New Berlin Day with antiques, crafts, and entertainment.

11.6 (1.3) *Where PA 304 bears right at "Y", bear left onto SR 3012.*

This country road soon crosses Sweitzer's Run. The Penns Creek Massacre, one of the earliest incidents of the French and Indian War, took place near here: a number of settlers were killed and the Leininger girls were captured by Indians.

13.8 (2.2) *Intersection with PA 104; go straight on SR 3012.*
　　　　Left here 0.3 mile, then left on Walnut Acres Road 0.6 mile is WALNUT ACRES (8–5 Mon.–Sat. except holidays), a large natural foods producer. In 1946 Paul and Betty Keene, former missionaries to India, started to farm simply and organically here, following Indian peasant practices. The natural foods business began when a jar of the Keenes' apple butter fell into the hands of a large eastern newspaper's food editor. Today the enterprise covers 450 acres and includes a bakery, a cannery, a freezery, and a retail outlet. Plant tours are given on weekdays. Visitors are also welcome to use a primitive campsite in the woods nearby.

The route continues through Wildwood, a group of turn-of-the-century cottages, then follows Penns Creek through a narrows darkened with hemlock.

14.9 (1.1) *"Y"; bear left onto Penns Creek Road.*
The route continues along Penns Creek. The wooded ridge sloping to the creek on the opposite side is Penns Creek Mountain, formed by a tough layer of quartzite.

17.4 (2.5) *Junction with SR 3004; turn left.*
The prosperity of these farms is indicated by their well-kept barns and their large blue Harvestore silos.

18.0 (0.6) *"Y"; bear left on SR 3004.*

18.4 (0.4) *Junction; turn left, then after 0.2 mile bear left at "Y" on SR 3004.*
The route again follows the tree-lined banks of clear Penns Creek, which offers swimming holes in several locations.

　　20.1 On the left is RED BRIDGE, a covered bridge built in 1855.

22.8 (4.4) *Intersection with PA 235 in Glen Iron; go straight on SR 3004.*
GLEN IRON, just to the right here, came to life when a railroad was built in 1876 and the village was made a depot. The three-story Glen Iron Hotel (now a private residence) and a store across the street are two of the railroad-era buildings. This location was also the site of the Berlin Iron Furnace, which began operating across Penns Creek in 1827. It functioned intermittently over the years, finally closing permanently in 1913.

25.5 (2.7) *Turn right on SR 3004.*

This is the "Tight End," where Penns Creek Mountain on the south and Paddy Mountain on the north come together, allowing only a narrow passageway for Penns Creek.

26.6 (1.1) *Junction with SR 3002; turn right.*

The rolling features on the floor of this valley are partly the result of a glacial prong which moved into the valley, then left piles of material when it receded.

30.1 LAURELTON, a crossroads hamlet, began when a gristmill was built on Laurel Run in 1839. Laurelton later benefited from the establishment of a woolen mill, but its major growth came in response to the logging industry that developed in the late 1800s.

The valley opens wider, filled with corn and hay fields bordered by hedgerows, spotted with large old farmsteads.

32.2 The low white frame building on the left is the Hartleton Mennonite Church.

32.5 (5.9) *Junction with PA 45 in Hartleton; turn right.*

HARTLETON got its name from Colonel Thomas Hartley, who established the community on land he received for his services during the Revolutionary War. Two pioneer roads converged here, making a good location for the tavern that was opened in 1793. The town expanded when a gravel turnpike was built through the valley in 1825. For many years Hartleton bustled with activity, but in 1875 the valley's railroad ignored Hartleton's wooings and took a route away from the town. Traffic that once used the turnpike switched to the railroad, and Hartleton dropped back to the sleepy village it is today.

32.9 (0.4) *Turn left onto SR 3003, passing Hartleton's post office.*

33.6 A white cinderblock Amish schoolhouse is on the right.

The wooded ridge bordering the valley ahead is marked with several open rocky slopes. These boulder fields are the result of extreme weather conditions near the glacial mass, which caused the rock forming the ridge to break off and fall onto the slope.

40.3 (7.4) *Junction with PA 45 in Mifflinburg; turn left.*

In the heart of Buffalo Valley, MIFFLINBURG is a small town of Georgian and Victorian architecture, much of it set directly on the town's narrow streets without the benefit of front yards. Mifflinburg is known as the "buggy town," because after the Civil War quality craftsmen turned the community into a renowned buggy- and sleigh-making center. At one time, as many as twenty shops existed here, most of them cottage industries, but a few were large employers. The Mifflinburg Buggy Company was the largest, with an annual production in 1903 of 1,500 vehicles. At the time the town's total annual production was estimated at 6,000. The products were marketed from New England to the Carolinas.

The automobile age changed all that in a few years, although for a while several shops produced truck and auto bodies. Proud citizens have opened the MIFFLINBURG BUGGY MUSEUM (June-September weekends, 717-966-0233; charge), comprising a restored shop, show room, and buggy maker's house. The town celebrates Buggy Day on the Saturday and Sunday before Memorial Day. The celebrations include buggy rides, arts and crafts demonstrations, displays of early machinery, traditional foods such as shoofly and raisin pies, musical events, and athletic competitions.

Overnight accommodations are available at the Mifflinburg Hotel (717-966-3003), an old stage stop inn. Its Scarlet D restaurant and bar has a brassy Victorian decor and offers three meals a day. An antique peanut roaster provides snacks for the bar.

41.1 (0.8) *Turn left onto the road to Forest Hill.*

41.6 (0.5) *Before the bridge, turn right onto Creek Road.*

42.3 (0.7) *Turn right onto SR 3009.*

44.6 (2.3) *Intersection with PA 192 in Cowan; turn right.*

47.1 In the hamlet of Buffalo Cross Roads is the Buffalo Presbyterian Church, an 1846 brick Greek Revival structure with a pedimented portico. The church sits in a grove of hemlocks.

PA 192 enters flatter and more fertile land as it nears the Susquehanna. At points views appear of the valley and of large, well-kept Pennsylvania barns.

49.4 Dockview Dairy on the left. Ice cream is made at the site.

51.1 (6.5) *Intersection with US 15; go straight onto Buffalo Road.*

51.3 (0.2) *Intersection with North Fourth Street; go straight onto St. Anthony Street.*

51.6 (0.3) *Turn right onto North Water Street.*

51.9 (0.3) *Junction with Market Street in Lewisburg.*

Bicycle Shops:
Bicycle Peddler, 20 N. Third Street, Lewisburg, (717) 524-4554

18 Ricketts Glen

- **Columbia and Luzerne Counties**
- **Start and end at Ricketts Glen State Park**
- **40.3 miles; flat to rolling with a few hills**
- **1 day**

During the Civil War rumors spread that the Confederates had broken through Union lines and built a fort on the rocky ramparts of North Mountain, aided by Southern sympathizers from the upper branches of Fishing Creek. A detachment of a thousand Union soldiers went to North Mountain, passing through Benton with bands playing, banners waving, and with cavalry, infantry, and artillery in proper marching order. The troops searched the mountain thoroughly for the fort and its reported two field pieces, brass cannon, and five-hundred inhabitants, but they found only a group of startled berry pickers.

0.0 (0.0) *Leaving the parking area for Ricketts Glen picnic area on PA 118, turn left onto PA 118.*

Above this picnic area, RICKETTS GLEN cuts into the Allegheny Front, the steep and rugged edge of the highlands. Descending 1,000 feet in three miles, Kitchen Creek tumbles over twenty-five waterfalls amid 500-year-old pines, hemlocks, and oaks. The glen was made when Kitchen Creek was forced to carve a new course over the Allegheny Front after its former channel became blocked by the melting ice sheet's earth and rocks.

The main set of waterfalls begins about two miles up the glen and can be reached by a trail. Just a few hundred feet on the other side of the highway, however, is Adams Falls, the glen's final falls, where a red rock precipice has been worn into smooth shapes by the rushing water.

RICKETTS GLEN STATE PARK (717-477-5675) was formerly the estate of Colonel Robert Bruce Ricketts. The main park area is on the top of the mountain at glacially formed Lake Jean, where a sand beach and lakeside camping areas with hot showers are provided. Camping reservations are accepted.

1.6 Red Rock, a crossroads hamlet with a few frame buildings, was named for the local shale bedrock. Here PA 487 leads steeply up Red Rock Mountain to the state park main area.

PA 118 follows along the base of the Allegheny Front, with views to the right of the front—here known as Red Rock Mountain or North Mountain—looming high above the valley floor.

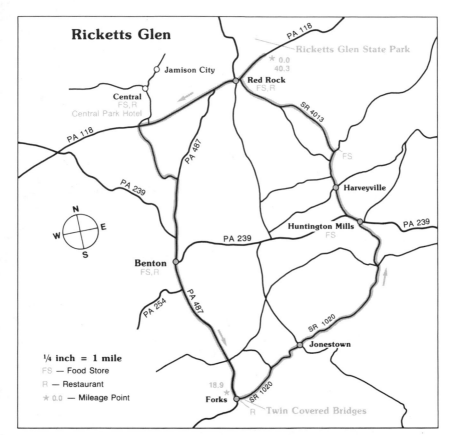

6.0 (6.0) *Intersection with the road to Central; turn left.*
    Right on this road 1.7 miles, along the West Branch of Fishing Creek, is CENTRAL, a village cupped by North Mountain. A sportsmen's resort, the place has many summer homes and the Central Park Hotel (717-925-6650), a three-story hunter's hotel with a bunk room and rooms with or without baths. The hotel's dining room and bar are notable for the many animal trophies and old hunting pieces that hang from the walls and ceilings. The hotel is open seven days a week year-round; lunch and dinner are served through the week; breakfast is offered on Sunday.

9.1 (3.1) *Junction with PA 487; turn right.*
    12.5 BENTON, a small town of large frame houses, is situated on the valley floor along Fishing Creek. The town was settled before 1800 as a farming community, but it prospered during the logging boom of the late 1800s as a center for lumber planing and wagon building. At the turn of the century the town supported three hotels.

Benton's original buildings and much of its prosperity disappeared in 1910 when a July Fourth fire, started by boys playing with fireworks, consumed much of the town. Most of the people were away enjoying the holiday, so few were present to fight the blaze. At the end of the day families returned to find their homes charred ruins.

Benton today is a minor commercial center and bedroom community. Its chief watering spot, the Benton Hotel, draws a clientele of bearded cowboys who arrive in jacked-up pickup trucks equipped with CBs and gun racks.

From Benton, PA 487 follows the wide level valley of Fishing Creek, past farms made prosperous by the fertile soils of this flood plain.

15.7 The STILLWATER COVERED BRIDGE, built in 1849, crosses Fishing Creek on the left. These nineteenth-century bridges were covered primarily to protect their structures from the elements.

18.9 (9.8) *Forks; turn left over a bridge onto the road to Jonestown (SR 1020).*

19.2 Now part of a small picnic area, TWIN COVERED BRIDGES on the right probably became twins when the stream channel changed and a new bridge was required. There is a small swimming hole in the stream.

20.3 The JOSIAH HESS COVERED BRIDGE is a short distance down a road on the left.

21.0 (2.1) *"Y"; bear right onto the road to Jonestown.*

The route follows partially farmed Huntington Creek valley. On its far side, the creek brushes against wooded Huntington Mountain, the first of the ridges that make up the Anthracite Region. It is the product of folding during the building of the Appalachians. To the north, the Allegheny Plateau contains the same rock layers left undisturbed. The coal on the plateau is bituminous or soft, but the coal in the southern region, hardened by the folding's pressure, is called anthracite.

The area between the plateau and the ridges through which this tour travels was once a high point in the topography, containing layers of coal, but over thousands of years it has been eroded to a rolling lowland. The terrain was made more uneven when the glacier dumped piles of sand, gravel, and rock here. Huntingdon Creek has cut down into this easily eroded material.

22.7 (1.7) *Intersection in Jonestown; go straight onto SR 1020.*

In the early 1800s JONESTOWN was important as a stop along

the Berwick Turnpike. In 1808 construction of the road commenced through a wilderness area to connect Berwick, Pennsylvania with Elmira, New York. Today parts of the turnpike are local roads, while others have become mere trails.

In 1815 the post office at Jonestown was named Fishing Creek, even though it was on Huntington Creek. Connecticut Yankee settlers had named the stream after the Connecticut governor and signer of the Declaration of Independence, Samuel Huntington. But the post office was given its name by Pennsylvanians who were still incensed over Connecticut's earlier claim to northern Pennsylvania. The controversy, based on overlapping land grants, saw some skirmishes. It was finally legally settled in the late 1700s.

30.1 (7.4) *Junction with PA 239 in Huntington Mills; turn left.*

HUNTINGTON MILLS, a rural village on Huntington Creek, has a hardware store, a grocery store, and a post office. Near the post office is a three-story gristmill, now vacant. Starting in 1775, Connecticut farmers settled here and brought with them New England architecture and town planning. Some of the homes are one-and-a-half-story frame buildings. Others are simple Georgian structures, similar in style to the Pennsylvania German homes but different because of surrounding yards. An unusual style for Pennsylvania is a salt box home, situated where the route enters the village.

Saltbox house in Huntington Mills, an example of New England architecture brought by Yankee settlers.

30.7 (0.6) *"Y"; bear right onto the road to Harveyville.*

31.9 In the hamlet of Harveyville is a one-and-a-half-story gristmill with a gambrel roof.

33.4 (2.7) *Turn left onto the road to Red Rock (SR 4013).*

The route passes through a wooded area in the small narrow valley of Kitchen Creek.

38.1 View to the right through trees of the mountainous Allegheny Front.

38.8 (5.4) *Junction with PA 118 in Red Rock; turn right.*

PA 487, intersecting PA 118 in Red Rock, is another part of the Berwick Turnpike.

40.3 (1.5) *Ricketts Glen State Park picnic area.*

Bicycle Shops:
None on route. The nearest shops are in Bloomsburg and Kingston.

Anthracite

Piles of black mine waste sparsely covered with scrub birch overlook conjested valley communities. Among the scarred mountains are "patches," collections of similar old houses, former mining company towns. Sometimes a huge decaying breaker, in which coal was processed, stands nearby. Above the pastel architecture of the larger towns rise gold onion-dome spires of Greek and Russian Catholic churches.

Even though the last wave of immigration—mostly from eastern Europe—ended some fifty years ago, the Anthracite region has kept a strong ethnic character. To this day, old people can go to a Ukrainian Orthodox church or a Lithuanian Catholic church and hear services in their native languages. These churches often hold bazaars selling food such as Polish pierogies (small potato-filled turnovers) or haluskies (cabbage pastries). Ethnic festivals, like Lithuanian Day or the Grand Irish Jubilee at Lakewood Park near Barnesville, have traditional music and folk dancing along with old country cooking.

The coal that brought these immigrants began forming hundreds of millions of years ago when Pennsylvania was a shallow sea. At times sand and clay from nearby mountains settled to the sea's bottom. At other times luxuriant plant growth in swampy water formed layers of peat. After these various layers had slowly turned to rock, they were squeezed and folded by the building of the Appalachian Mountains. The pressure was so great that the layers of peat, now no longer horizontal, were changed to hard coal or anthracite. Several hundred million years of erosion washed away the anthracite in many places, but it could not remove these fields which were protected by the deep, tight folding.

Mining of hard coal began in the early 1800s, first by Welsh and Cornish miners, then Irishmen and Germans, and finally eastern Europeans late in the century. Their labors fed America's power needs for a hundred years. Then debilitating strikes during the 1920s sent many customers elsewhere for fuel. Rising labor costs and increased mining costs for deeper, less accessible coal made anthracite expensive. Since World War II, conversion to oil and gas for home heating has intensified the industry's and the area's decline.

The anthracite region's scenery is often not pretty, its many ridges can make bicycling difficult, and its roads may be busy and narrow, especially in the heavily populated valleys. But carefully planned rides can avoid these problems and reveal the area's unique landscape and culture.

For More Information:
Carbon County Tourist Promotion Agency, 1004 Main Street, Stroudsburg, PA 18360, (717) 325-3673
Luzerne County Tourist Promotion Agency, 35 Denison Street, Forty Fort, PA 18704, (717) 288-6784
Northumberland County Tourist Promotion Agency, 370 Market Street, Room 411, Sunbury, PA 17801, (717) 988-4295
Schuylkill County Tourist Promotion Agency, 201 East Laurel Boulevard, Pottsville, PA 17901, (717) 622-7700

Area Bicycle Clubs:
Lackawanna Bicycle Club, 309 Thirteenth Street, Scranton, PA 18504
Wilkes-Barre Velo Club, P.O. Box 2491, Wilkes-Barre, PA 18703
Wyoming Valley Bicycle Club, P.O. Box 253, Dallas, PA 18612

St. Mary's Greek Orthodox Church in Freeland, an example of the ethnic diversity in this area of Pennsylvania.

19 Eckley

- **Luzerne and Carbon Counties**
- **Start and end at Hickory Run State Park**
- **28.1 miles; flat with some steep climbs**
- **1 day**

Early in this century, immigrant mining families in the anthracite coal fields faced hard work, privation, ill-treatment, and possible tragedy. Working conditions were the worst for new miners, because they got the lowest-paying and most dangerous jobs. For the old hands the work and pay improved, but every miner risked life and limb from small accidents as well as cave-ins and explosions. Mine inspection was cursory at best.

Even children were not spared the rigors and dangers of mining. Boys as young as nine spent their days bent over in the dusty breakers, picking out slate from coal in the chutes. At twelve they became door boys, manning mine tunnel doors and stopping coal cars by spragging—throwing a hardwood billet into the spokes. When they reached fourteen they joined their elders as laborers in the mines.

Families lived in cheap, crowded, and uncomfortable company housing and shopped at the company store. This dependency made them the pawn of the coal companies, which used high prices and low pay to keep them in debt and insure a steady supply of cheap labor.

Miners' wives were in charge of child rearing, household purchasing, cooking, and cleaning. Besides the immediate family, their responsibilities might extend to boarders and newly arrived relatives from the old country. Some wives did laundry or housework for extra money or went to work in one of the sweaty textile mills found throughout the anthracite region.

In spite of the hardships—or perhaps because of them—coal mining towns were known for their merrymaking. In communities dominated by Southern and Eastern Europeans, churches sponsored festivals on saints' days and other occasions, with sporting events, dancing, and generous eating and drinking. Ethnic brotherhoods also had their picnics and festivals. Weddings and christenings were always calls for celebration, as were weekly paydays, when men poured into their towns' many bars for a night of cards, music, talk, and drink.

0.0 (0.0) *Leaving the parking lot at the Hickory Run State Park office, turn left onto PA 534. (The Lehigh Tannery bridge is out until*

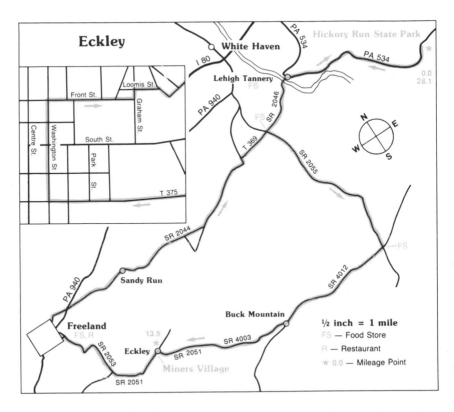

mid to late 1989; until then this tour must be started at a point on the other side of the Lehigh River, such as Freeland or Eckley.)

HICKORY RUN STATE PARK (717-443-9991), straddling the boundary between the Poconos and the Anthracite Region, is in a wooded hilly area. Once the site of logging operations, Hickory Run's park office and chapel were part of Hickory Run Village, a lumber camp. The park offers swimming at a sandy beach, camping (with showers) in a wooded area, and a camp store. Campground reservations are accepted for holiday weekends only.

The main attraction of Hickory Run State Park is a 1,800-foot-long boulder field, the largest of its kind in the eastern United States. The field, flat with rounded boulders of various sizes, was indirectly caused by continental glaciation. The glacier came within a mile of here, so close that freezing and thawing over a long period of time caused boulders to break from adjacent bedrock ridges. A mass of sand, clay, and ice carried the boulders to this plain and then melted and washed away at the end of the glacial period, leaving the boulders behind.

From Hickory Run to Tannery the route passes through a wooded area with a number of steep climbs, making this section the most difficult of the entire tour. It could be avoided by starting at Lehigh Tannery.

3.2 (3.2) *Lehigh Tannery; turn left onto SR 2046 and cross Lehigh River.*
Here the LEHIGH RIVER forms rapids as it winds its way through a rugged and remote gorge.

4.4 (1.2) *Intersection with SR 2055; turn left.*

8.1 (3.7) *Intersection with SR 4012; turn right.*

10.9 (2.8) *"Y" by a church in Buck Mountain; bear right onto SR 4003 (later SR 2051).*
After Buck Mountain, a former mining village with several abandoned buildings, the route climbs several hundred feet and enters a typical anthracite landscape of disrupted terrain, sulfur-colored waste piles, and scrub birch. This and the other side of Eckley are still being strip mined, and huge shovels (into which cars can drive), dump trucks (also monstrous), and other equipment are in operation.

13.5 (2.6) *Junction in Eckley; turn left on SR 2051.*
ECKLEY is one of hundreds of "patch towns" that coal companies built for their mining operations. Like others, Eckley consists of simple frame structures, similar in design and spaced evenly along the streets. However, Eckley was also the filming site of *The Molly Maguires,* a 1970 movie starring Sean Connery. The town returned to its nineteenth-century appearance by hiding wires and antennas, and by covering asphalt shingles with clapboard veneer. The film's black breaker, a huge structure meant for coal processing, looms above the town. It was supposed to burn in the movie, but an accidental fire in a nearby real breaker provided the needed footage.

Eckley is also distinctive because the Pennsylvania Historical and Museum Commission owns and runs it as a living museum. Retired miners, widows, or their children still live in homes which they now rent from the state instead of from the mining company. (Some question whether life is any better under the state's restrictions!)

Several buildings in the village are open to the public, including the Episcopal and Roman Catholic churches, the company store, and a double residence. At one end of town a modern VISITORS CENTER (9–5 Tues.–Sat., 12–5 Sun.; charge) features a

A house in the mining village of Eckley.

slide presentation and a museum depicting mining community life.

15.4 A view to the right over strip mines is of Freeland, with a skyline decorated by onion dome steeples.

16.0 (2.5) *Intersection in Highland; go straight onto SR 2053.*

16.3 (0.3) *Turn left onto T 375 (unmarked).*

16.7 (0.4) *Intersection with Washington Street in Freeland; turn right.*

FREELAND, a large town packed with buildings, sits on a plateau amid the spoil banks of strip mines. Its residences are the big white or pastel frame structures typical of larger anthracite towns. Many are double homes. Most buildings are well cared for, and the little back yards often hold vegetable and flower gardens.

Italian and Eastern European names dominate the business section.

The town grew to become a regional commercial center because it was not controlled by any coal company—hence its name. This opened it to private business, national churches, and bars. A recent count shows that the town, with a population of only about 5,000, supports thirteen churches and thirty-eight bars and clubs.

During August, Freeland holds its week-long Homecoming, when former residents return to see old friends and enjoy carnival rides, ethnic cooking, dancing, and sporting events such as boxing and baseball. Many people schedule summer vacations for the occasion, which draws several thousand visitors. A strong community spirit, demonstrated by events such as this, makes people who have lived away for years think of this old mining town as home. Many even insist on being buried here.

17.0 (0.3) *Intersection with Front Street; turn right.*

17.3 (0.3) *Junction with Graham Street; turn left, then immediately right onto Loomis Street.*

17.4 (0.1) *Junction; turn right onto an unmarked street.*

19.2 Sandy Run is a patch town with a few homes remaining. These sport asphalt and aluminum siding.

After Sandy Run the route descends, leaves the coal-bearing rock formations, and moves into a mostly wooded area with some farming.

23.0 (5.6) *Immediately after crossing a bridge, turn right onto T 369 (unmarked road).*

24.9 (1.9) *Junction with PA 534 in Lehigh Tannery; turn right.*

28.1 (3.2) *Hickory Run State Park.*

Bicycle Shops:
None on route. The nearest shop is in Hazelton.

Poconos

The Pocono Mountains are not mountains; the region is actually a forested plateau, occasionally dissected by narrow streams. For years it has been a much-touted recreation area with large resorts, children's summer camps, and honeymoon motels featuring heart-shaped pools, heart-shaped beds, and heart-shaped bathtubs. The area's popularity, especially with nearby New Yorkers, comes in part from its high elevation which brings cool summers and snowy winters. This elevation, obviously unpopular with farmers, explains the miles of forest as well as the pockets of balsam fir, tamarack, and black spruce ordinarily found farther north.

Resorts, camps, and second home developments border many of the region's lakes. Long ago when the great ice sheets disappeared, boulders, sand, and other matter left behind plugged valleys, creating lakes, swamps, and bogs. Diverted streams also found their way over rough slopes, especially along the Poconos' eastern escarpment, forming spectacular waterfalls, another of the region's natural attractions.

Although parts of the Poconos, especially in the western half, are heavily commercialized, much forest scenery remains. Roads on top of the plateau are nearly flat, but difficult climbing is sometimes necessary on roads that leave stream valleys. Since this is a resort area, there are innumerable hotels and motels in the Poconos, along with other tourist accommodations.

For More Information:
Pocono Mountain Vacation Bureau, 1004 Main Street, Stroudsburg, PA 18360, (800) 762-6667

Area Bicycle Club:
Lackawanna Bicycle Club, 309 Thirteenth Street, Scranton, PA 18504

20 Bushkill

- **Pike and Monroe Counties**
- **Start and end at George W. Childs Picnic Area
  (west of Dingmans Ferry on SR 2004)**
- **42.1 miles; flat to rolling with some climbs**
- **1 day**

In the late 1700s the Delaware River flowed through a wild and remote area. Despite the rigors of wilderness life and the danger of savages, settlements started up at locations where the fertile flood plain of the river provided good farmland, and where streams falling steeply off the Pocono Escarpment provided water power for milling. Manuel Gonzales was one of the first settlers at what was to become Bushkill, near the famed Bushkill Falls.

Gonzales had seven daughters and each helped with the chores. On one occasion Elizabeth, seven years old, was helping her father round up some horses that had wandered onto the flats along the river. Suddenly from the woods sprang a party of Indians. Manuel jumped into a river washout and was concealed, but Lizzie became separated from her father and was seized by the Indians. Her father heard her scream as the Indians fled into the forest.

That night at their encampment, the Indians debated what to do with Elizabeth. One respected old Indian noted that she was a smart girl and volunteered to raise her as his own. Elizabeth was taken to Canada where she lived as an Indian with a tribe. She married an Indian chief and bore him two children.

Thirty-two years after the incident, when Indian troubles had subsided, an old man came to Bushkill and sought out Manuel Gonzales. The man said that if Gonzales would give him a mug of cider he would tell Gonzales the whereabouts of his long-lost daughter. Manuel complied and listened in amazement to the man's description of his daughter and her circumstances.

Soon afterward Gonzales and a neighbor traveled to Canada and found Elizabeth. She remembered that her name was Lizzie, that she had lived by a large river, and she recalled certain incidents of her childhood. Even though her husband and children had died, she was reluctant to leave the Indian life she had known so long. At last her father prevailed upon her. She returned to Bushkill, married again, and lived there the rest of her life.

0.0 (0.0) *Leaving the parking area of the George W. Childs Picnic Area, turn right onto SR 2004.*

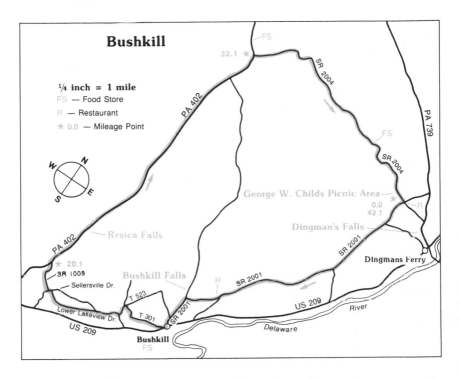

The GEORGE W. CHILDS PICNIC AREA, formerly a state park, now belongs to the U.S. Park Service. Here Dingman's Creek forms three falls in a hemlock-shaded glen.

0.4 (0.4) *Intersection with SR 2001; turn right.*

1.7 Johnny Bee Road joins on the left.

On this road steeply downhill 1.7 miles, then left on the entrance road 0.7 mile, is DINGMAN'S FALLS (9–5 weekdays, 9–7 weekends; free), the highest falls in Pennsylvania. Dingman's Creek falls 177 feet over beds of shale, siltstone, and sandstone. Here also is SILVERTHREAD FALLS, a thin stream of water falling through a narrow rock fracture. Once private, the site is now administered as part of the Delaware Water Gap National Recreation Area.

4.5 (4.1) *"Y"; bear right on SR 2001.*

The route runs on top of the flat Pocono Plateau through an area of young woods, overgrown fields, and former farms. Tumbledown stone walls in the woods along the road tell of fields that were abandoned long ago. Farming is difficult in the poor glacial soil and the high elevations here. Lately the land has become desirable for second home developments, and several appear along this portion of the tour.

9.8 (5.3) *"Y"; bear right on SR 2001.*

11.2 (1.4) *Junction; turn left on SR 2001.*

Right here 0.2 mile is BUSHKILL FALLS, (spring-fall, 8–dusk daily; charge), known as the Niagara of Pennsylvania. Although the glen contains a number of stupendous waterfalls, the site is commercially operated, and to get to the falls one must pass a miniature golf course and a group of cottages containing animal toys, Pennsylvania Dutch gifts, an assortment of printed T-shirts, and other gimcracks and doodads.

12.7 (1.5) *Junction with US 209 in Bushkill; turn right, then right again just before a bridge.*

BUSHKILL, consisting now of a few buildings, was once larger, but many structures were removed when the Army Corps of Engineers readied the area to be flooded by the Tocks Island Dam. The Vietnam War prevented the Corps from continuing this project, and in the meantime environmentalists have been able to stop it completely. The Delaware River has been placed in the Wild and Scenic Rivers category, to be preserved in its natural state. At the time of the dam project, the district was made a National Recreation Area, which it remains today.

This road follows Bushkill Creek in a wooded area. "Bushkill" is Dutch for little river, a reminder of the Delaware's early Dutch settlement.

15.0 (2.3) *Junction; turn left onto T 523 (unmarked).*

15.4 (0.4) *Junction with Lower Lakeview Drive; turn right.*

Along this road on the left is an area of small lakes and dry depressions. These are all "kettles," produced when blocks of ice from the glacier were covered with sand and gravel and then melted, leaving depressions on the earth's surface that sometimes filled with water.

16.5 View to left of the Delaware Valley. New Jersey's Kittatinny Mountain is the ridge in the distance.

18.7 (3.3) *Junction with Sellersville Drive; turn left, then immediately right onto the road to Resica Falls.*

20.1 (1.4) *Junction with PA 402; turn right.*

PA 402 slowly climbs to the top of the plateau. Much of the roadside is state forest and has been preserved from development.

22.1 On the right is the Resica Falls Scout Reservation which includes RESICA FALLS, open to the public and only a short distance from the highway. This waterfall once powered a tannery

Dingman's Falls, the highest in Pennsylvania.

which was the center of a small community. The mill race is still visible, carved in the bedrock where a trail leads to the falls. A stone schoolhouse remains, along with remnants of other buildings. The scouts have a picnic area at the falls.

Resica Falls, like other waterfalls along the Pocono Escarpment, is the result of a stream being diverted by glacier-dumped matter. Since these are relatively young streams they have not yet worn a gentle gradient, and outcrops of harder rock still exist, forming falls.

32.1 (12.0) *After Porters Lake, turn right onto the road to Childs Park.*

Porters Lake is one of many lakes on the Pocono Plateau which owe their existence to continental glaciation. Many have filled with sediment and become swamps. But some of those have been dammed by man and turned back into lakes. Dammed or natural, the lakes are popular spots for second-home developments and summer camps.

The route continues through open woods past occasional groups of white frame cottages. Beyond the state forest, second home developments appear set in the woods, with names like Pocono Estates or Pocono Lakes or Pocono Village.

42.1 (10.0) *George W. Childs Picnic Area.*

Bicycle Shops:
None on route. The nearest shops are in Stroudsburg and East Stroudsburg.

21 Lackawaxen River

- **Wayne and Pike Counties**
- **Start and end at Hawley**
- **48.4 miles; flat to rolling with a few climbs**
- **1 or 2 days; overnight stop at Kittatinny Campgrounds (mile 18.7) or Rebers Motel (mile 21.2)**

In 1842 Horace Greeley, famous publisher of the New York *Tribune*, founded a colony based on the ideas of Utopian Socialist Francois Marie Charles Fourier. Greeley organized and financed the Sylvania Society, which purchased several thousand acres of land on the Pocono Plateau and built there an immense frame structure containing living quarters, work rooms, a common dining hall, and a social hall. According to Fourier's thinking, the community was to be self-sufficient; all would share in the property and the labor.

The commune ran into trouble when a number of rich and prominent New York City families decided to use the colony as a reformatory for their wayward sons. They bought stock in the enterprise and shipped off the troublesome and lazy lads to the Poconos.

Greeley later claimed that the place could only raise stones and snakes. The first year's crop was inadequate. And the land did have many rattlesnakes: once a colonist brought in seventeen. One was so large that slippers were made from it and presented to Mr. Greeley on his next visit.

In spite of the bad boys, the poor crops, and the rattlesnakes, the bulk of the membership held out for a second year. Good markets had been found for the community's leather shoes and wooden wagons. Plantings were doubled to insure a sufficient yield. All looked promising until a freak July Fourth frost in 1845 left the garden, fields, and orchards a blackened wasteland. In a few days not a soul remained.

0.0 (0.0) *Junction of US 6 and PA 590 in Hawley; head east on PA 590.*

HAWLEY is a small town straddling busy US Route 6. Its first spurt of growth occurred when the Delaware and Hudson Canal was completed in 1820. The canal, a private venture, ran 108 miles from Eddyville at the Hudson River to Honesdale in the north and was built to carry coal from the northern coal fields. At Honesdale a gravity railroad, with stationary engines pulling cars up inclined planes, connected with Carbondale and the mines. A canal basin

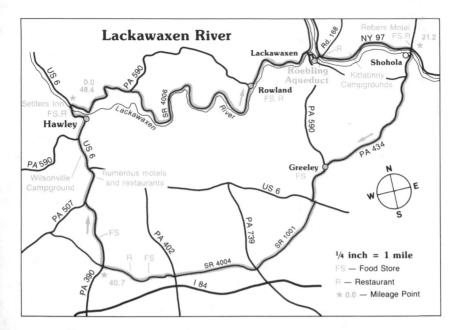

built at Hawley is now a playing field in Bingham Park. Greek Revival buildings of the canal era are situated nearby, along PA 590.

In 1850 the Pennsylvania Coal Company built another gravity railroad from Hawley to Port Griffith on the Susquehanna. There were twenty-two inclined planes, powered mostly by steam but in four cases by waterwheels. The Pennsylvania Coal Company sold coal to the Delaware and Hudson Canal until the 1860s, when the company built its own parallel locomotive line to Lackawaxen. The Pioneer Coach, a passenger car on the Gravity Railroad, is on display near Hawley's library.

Today the economy of Hawley is based largely on tourism because of its location on the edge of the Poconos and its nearness to Lake Wallenpaupack, a nine-square-mile artificial lake. The lake was built in 1926 by the Pennsylvania Power and Light Company.

Across from Bingham Park is Settler's Inn (717-226-2993), a Tudor Revival structure with a rustic decor. Rooms have bathrooms and are pleasantly furnished. Lunch and dinner are available in the dining room, which is decorated with old farm implements and other relics.

3.4 (3.4) *Bear right onto the road to Kimbles.*

  4.5 Across the valley on the right is a green cylindrical tower on the rocky hillside. This is a surge tank which acts as a shock absorber when the velocity of water rushing through a flume from Lake Wallenpaupack is changed abruptly. Two pipes leaving the bottom of the surge tank carry water to two turbines where electricity is made.

The route descends to the LACKAWAXEN RIVER and follows its shoreline through a remote wooded area to the Delaware River. Old stone walls and depressions are all that remain of the Delaware and Hudson Canal. Some of the old frame homes through here were lockkeepers' houses. The canal was abandoned in 1898.

The Lackawaxen River is a swift-moving stream. Occasionally signs along the road warn of rapidly changing river levels. At Lake Wallenpaupack water is discharged at irregular intervals for electricity production.

12.8 (9.4) *Rowlands; go straight onto PA 590.*

Zane Grey described the Lackawaxen as "a little river hidden away . . . dashing white sheeted over ferny cliffs, wine-brown where the whirling pools suck the stain from the hemlock roots . . . [and] harbor the speckled trout."

16.4 (3.6) *After crossing Lackawaxen River, turn left onto the road into Lackawaxen.*

16.7 On the right and facing the Delaware River is the ZANE GREY MUSEUM (Apr. 15–Sept. 15, 10–4 Tues.–Sun.; charge), the two-story frame home of Zane Grey, early-twentieth-century western novel writer. It was here on his favorite fishing river that Grey met his wife-to-be and wrote his first novel. The museum holds memorabilia; Zane Grey and his wife are buried in a nearby cemetery.

Lackawaxen is a village of scattered turn-of-the-century frame homes, many facing the Delaware.

17.0 (0.6) *Turn left and cross the Delaware River on the Roebling Aqueduct.*

The ROEBLING AQUEDUCT once carried the canal over the Delaware River. As part of a general enlargement of the canal, it was designed and constructed between 1847 and 1850 by John A. Roebling, builder of the Brooklyn Bridge. Previously, canal boats had crossed the river by rope ferry in slack water created by a dam. As cargo increased on the canal, this became more and more of a bottleneck, slowing down traffic in good weather and stopping it during high water. Furthermore, the slack water and canal traffic obstructed rafts on the Delaware, bringing the anger of raftsmen upon the Delaware and Hudson Company.

The company accepted Roebling's suspension design because it was the least expensive proposed and because it would require only three piers, allowing more room for rafts and river debris to pass beneath. The structure, which once held 1,900 tons of water, is supported by two-and-a-half-inch cables consisting of 2,150 iron wires. It is considered the oldest standing suspension bridge in the United States.

After the canal was abandoned, the aqueduct was made into a private toll bridge, and it kept that function until the National Park Service purchased it in 1980. It has since been renovated and reopened for vehicles.

17.1 (0.1) *Junction with NY 97; turn right.*
From here Sullivan County Road 168 leads uphill 0.8 mile to MINISINK BATTLEGROUND PARK where the Battle of Minisink was fought on July 22, 1779. Several days before, civilized and scholarly Joseph Brant, an Indian, had led a party of Tories and Indians in the destruction of Minisink (now Port Jervis). A volunteer militia pursued them to this point. Most of the militiamen were killed, but the survivors are said to have escaped when an officer accidently gave the Masonic distress signal and Brant, a Mason, let them flee into the forest.

18.7 Kittatinny Campgrounds (914-557-8611), along the Delaware River, is also a canoe camp and livery. The campground has riverside sites, showers, a camp store, and a swimming pool.

NY 92 follows along the Delaware River. The road is very busy on summer weekends when urbanites come here to canoe. Canoe liveries are a multi-million-dollar business on the river. Thousands of canoes a day pass through this section.

21.2 (4.1) *Barryville; turn right and go over a bridge, then go straight onto PA 434.*

The Roebling Aqueduct over the Delaware River, the oldest suspension bridge still standing in the United States.

Barryville, a New York State village, has true New York culture—a sandwich labeled a sub or a hoagie in Pennsylvania is a grinder here.

Rebers Motel (914-557-6222) has motel units and a dining room.

21.5 Shohola, a short distance to the right, was a railroad tourist stop during the mid-1800s. A car from the gravity railroad in Hawley carried passengers to nearby Shohola Glen, now closed to the public.

PA 434 gently climbs through a wooded valley to the top of the Pocono Plateau. Cottages are scattered along the road.

28.0 GREELEY, a village of large former boarding houses, was the site of Horace Greeley's commune. The present community was established by Germans who continued to speak their native language as late as 1930.

29.6 (8.4) *Junction with US 6; turn left, then immediately right onto SR 1001*

Now in deciduous forest on top of the fairly flat plateau, the route passes several entrances to Pocono Mountains second-home developments, including "Camelot Forest Mobile and Modular Home Community."

33.6 At this intersection, known as Lords Valley, is the Lord House, a private home which was once a hotel kept for stage route travelers by Levi Lord and his sons.

40.7 (11.1) *Intersection with PA 390; turn right.*

PA 390 descends through a wooded area of summer homes.

43.7 (3.0) *Junction with PA 507; turn right.*

45.2 (1.5) *Junction with US 6; turn left.*

Motels, restaurants, and tourist shops do business along US 6.

45.8 Wilsonville Recreation and Camping Area (717-226-4382) is on the left along Lake Wallenpaupack. The camping area has a small store and showers. A public swimming beach is available.

46.2 The road on the left leads a short distance to LAKE WALLENPAUPACK DAM OVERLOOK and the Pennsylvania Power and Light visitors center.

48.4 (3.2) *Hawley.*

Bicycle Shops:
None on route. The nearest shop is in Honesdale.

Northeast

The northeastern corner of Pennsylvania is a rural area, a patchwork of fields and woodlots and small towns spread over rolling hills. Because it is part of the Appalachian Plateau, an area of flat-lying bedrock left undisturbed by the building of the Appalachians, the Northeast lacks the limestone lowlands, long parallel ridges, and rugged mountains found in other parts of the state. The northeastern hills were simply made by streams slowly cutting the valleys away.

Glaciers covered northern Pennsylvania thousands of years ago during the ice age. When the ice sheets receded, they left behind sand, stones, and boulders which contributed to the hilliness of this area and made soils poor for farming. Glacial deposits also filled valleys, disrupting stream patterns and forming lakes. Lakes, ponds, and swamps especially abound in eastern Susquehanna County and northern Wayne County.

Coming from similar glaciated country, Connecticut Yankees settled northeastern Pennsylvania during the late 1700s and early 1800s. In fact, this area was part of Connecticut as well as of Pennsylvania, because King Charles II gave overlapping deeds to the two colonies. During several skirmishes known as the Yankee-Pennemite Wars, Pennsylvanians used military force to oust the Yankees. After Pennsylvania became a state, legal action finally settled the dispute.

The Yankees, however, stayed and gave northeastern Pennsylvania its New England flavor. They built towns with greens and Greek Revival architecture. Their interest in the ancient democracies also inspired town names such as Athens, Troy, and Rome, and they added New Englandish names such as New Milford, East Smithfield, and Windham Center. Their rural architecture was predominantly wooden houses, and barns lacking the overhang of Pennsylvania German barns farther south. And with the glacial stones in their fields, farmers made walls just as they had in New England.

The Northeast has many little-travelled country roads that pass through bucolic farmland and picturesque villages. Many of the state highways are also relatively free of traffic. However, except where the roads follow streams, their courses over one hill after another can mean strenuous bicycling.

For More Information:
Endless Mountains Association (Bradford, Susquehanna, and Sullivan Coun-

ties), R.D. 6, Box 132A, Tunkhannock, PA 18657, (717) 836-5431

Area Bicycle Club:
Southern Tier Bicycle Club, 4009 Drexel Drive, Binghamton, NY 13903

Greek Revival style church at Sheshequin.

22 Susquehanna County

- **Susquehanna County**
- **Start and end at Lenox (Interstate 81 Exit 64)**
- **63.6 miles; flat to rolling with some climbs**
- **1 or 2 days; overnight stop at Jefferson Inn (mile 33.6)**

Blackman's 1873 *History of Susquehanna County* contains an account of Joseph Smith, founder of the Mormon Church, who lived in the county before and during—as the book puts it—"the compilation or, rather, the translation of the Book of Mormon." Locals interviewed for the book claimed that Smith spent much time searching for buried treasure and persuaded others to join him. To find the treasures' locations, Smith would look into a hat containing a "seeing stone" which he had purchased from a neighbor. The neighbor's little boy had won local fame using the rock to find lost articles and missing children. The testimony of Smith's father-in-law adds that using this rock, or "peeping," was Smith's method for translating the plates he had brought from Palmyra, New York.

Circumstances always prevented Joseph Smith from actually finding treasure. Once he talked a wealthy farmer into financing a digging operation. When nothing appeared after much work Smith declared that an "enchantment" had moved the treasure and that it was necessary to sacrifice a perfectly white dog and sprinkle its blood on the ground. Smith and the farmer searched for such an animal but none could be found. Smith finally decided a white sheep would do, so they got one and spread its blood as directed. When further digging proved fruitless, Smith answered the angry farmer "that the Almighty was displeased with them for attempting to palm off on Him a white sheep for a white dog, and had allowed the enchantment to remove the treasure."

0.0 (0.0) *Intersection of PA 106 and PA 92 in Lenox; head north on PA 92.*

PA 92 follows the valley of Tunkhannock Creek, passing through fields and pastures bordered by wooded hills. Glacial melt waters widened this valley; earth and rock brought here by the glacier made the rolling topography and the poor stony soil.

Yankee settlers improved these lands by removing the stones to build fences—just as they had done in Massachusetts and Connecticut. In their spare time, boys would pile stones at the fields' edges. Later, someone would build a fence for 75 cents a

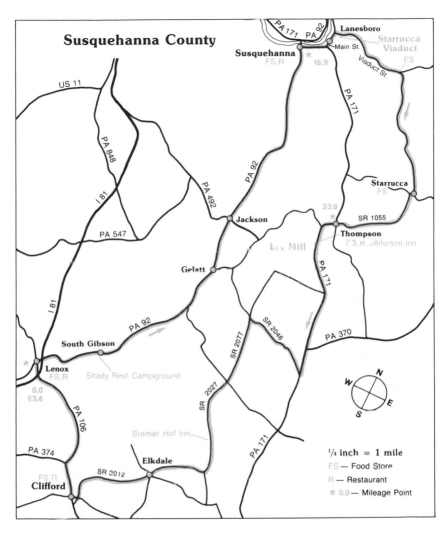

rod. During the 1930s many of the walls were taken apart and the stone used to pave local roads.

New England farmers also brought their architecture, still evident among the farms and villages of the valley. Their barns are small and lack the overhang typical of southeastern Pennsylvania's German barns. A number of the homes have gable-end fronts and attached wings. Greek Revival features, giving buildings a temple-like appearance, mark the older homes. One good example of Greek Revival design is the former Jackson Methodist Church, a small white building with a pedimented gable, and an entrance with flanking pilasters and an overhead entablature.

18.9 (18.9) *Junction in Susquehanna; turn right, then go straight onto PA 171.*

SUSQUEHANNA, a town with a winding main street and side streets leading steeply uphill, grew at a point on the Susquehanna River where the Erie Railroad built its repair shops. Here, where frame residences spread up the hillsides, "you go uphill to go down into your cellar." Like most late-nineteenth-century railroad towns, many of the brick commercial buildings are three or four stories tall and have Victorian ornamentation on their facades.

Now the repair shops are gone from the middle of town, replaced by a small shopping center. The railroad's decline hurt the town; store fronts are vacant and several homes are boarded up. But Susquehanna's proximity to New York's industrial Binghamton has made it a bedroom community.

At one end of town is the STARRUCCA HOUSE, one of the few railroad depots in America combined with a hotel and restaurant. This huge red brick building has pointed-arch windows, a walkway overhang supported by arched brackets, and other features of the Victorian Gothic style. On the National Register of Historic Places, it is open as a restaurant and is being refurnished as a hotel.

The owner of the Starrucca House, a local entrepreneur, intends to return the building to its former grandeur. A second floor has been removed at one end to give the old ballroom its full height and to reveal an arched beam ceiling.

Across the river from Susquehanna is Oakland, once the home of Joseph Smith and the place where he wrote the Book of Mormon. Here Smith and a cohort were visited by John the Baptist as well as by the Apostles Peter, James, and John, who conferred upon the two men various orders of priesthood. The Church of Jesus Christ of Latter-Day Saints commemorates these events with an impressive monument 1.9 miles west of Oakland on PA 171.

20.1 (1.2) *Where PA 171 turns right, go straight under a bridge and into Lanesboro on Main Street.*

20.7 (0.6) *Turn right onto Viaduct Street and pass under Starrucca Viaduct.*

Spanning 1,000 feet across Starrucca Creek valley and one hundred feet above this road, the STARRUCCA VIADUCT carries locomotives today just as it did after it was built in 1848. The bridge is made of locally quarried stone that was cut to size, numbered, then carried to the site and fit into place. The first engine to cross the bridge is supposed to have made the trip unmanned because the engineers were afraid the structure would collapse. The viaduct is on the National Register of Historic Places.

29.6 (8.9) *Starrucca; turn right over a bridge, then immediately left onto the road to Thompson (SR 1005).*

The route follows Starrucca Creek along a sparsely populated valley. Farms are small, often in disrepair, and fields are overgrown with weeds and shrubs—showing how hard it is to farm these poor glacial soils.

33.6 (4.0) *Intersection in Thompson; go straight onto PA 171.*

THOMPSON, a pleasant community of large frame houses and wide lawns, sits amid farmland near the top of the Allegheny Plateau. The village blossomed when the new Jefferson Railroad located a station here in 1871, creating an important center for the surrounding rural population.

The R.E. LEE AND SONS MILL on PA 171 is one of the few water-powered feed mills still in commercial operation. Water backed up by a dam falls through a forty-foot flume and turns a turbine which is connected by belts to the mill's equipment. Grain from all over the nation is ground and blended according to each farmer's specifications.

At the southern edge of Thompson, across from the Texaco station on PA 171, is Stoney's Diner—locally known as Flo's. There

Starrucca Viaduct, the oldest operating stone arched railroad bridge in the United States.

is no sign. Flo has furnished the place with chairs and tables from various sources. Knick-knacks fill shelves and window sills. In one corner is a 3-D picture of the Last Supper. Flo, a grandmotherly type, waits, cooks, and serves food in portions that would not match their prices anywhere else.

The Jefferson Inn (717-727-2625) is a white clapboard building with blue shutters and a two-story front porch. Built at the time of the railroad's construction, it sits across from Thompson's now-vacant depot. The inn serves meals and has plainly furnished rooms.

Past Thompson the route follows PA 171 through woods and fields on top of the Allegheny Plateau. Low wooded mountains can be seen in the distance on the left. These are Sugarloaf Mountain and Mount Ararat, the northern tip of the folded rock structure which forms the crescent-shaped Wyoming Basin of Scranton and Wilkes-Barre.

40.7 (7.1) *Turn right onto the road to Gelatt (SR 2046).*

Fiddle Lake, one of the many glacial lakes in the area, is rimmed with cottages.

44.1 (3.4) *Intersection after Fiddle Lake; turn left onto SR 2077 (later SR 2027).*

This little-used country road is said to be the highest in the county. At one point there is a vista to the west of the rolling hills covered with a patchwork of fields and forests characteristic of this region. Later, the road passes around ELK HILL, a blemish on the fairly flat plateau and the result of the ancient collision that formed the Appalachians. Ski slopes stripe the mountainside and chalets dot the surrounding fields.

53.4 (9.3) *Elkdale; cross a bridge, then turn right onto the road to Clifford (SR 2012).*

57.0 (3.6) *Intersection; turn right into Clifford, then turn right onto PA 106.*

63.6 (6.6) *Lenox.*

Bicycle Shops:
None on route. The nearest shops are in Scranton, Pennsylvania, and Binghamton, New York.

23 North Branch

- **Bradford County**
- **Start and end at Wysox**
- **46 miles; flat to rolling with a few climbs**
- **1 or 2 days; overnight stop at Hotel Wyalusing (mile 14.4) or Merryall Park Campground (mile 17.2)**

Shortly after it enters Pennsylvania, the North Branch of the Susquehanna River winds its way among wooded hills and bottom-land fields, forming at one point a horseshoe-shaped peninsula. Here in the fall of 1792 an illustrious group of Frenchmen—some minor nobility, some courtiers to the King, others wealthy plantation owners from Santo Domingo—stepped ashore to build a refuge far away from the turmoil of revolutionary France and the slave uprisings of the West Indies. Besides concern for their own safety, it is believed they wanted to make French Azilum home for their beloved Queen, Marie Antoinette.

For nearly a decade this "Paris in the Wilderness" grew as more exiles arrived. Eventually there were fifty log buildings including a distillery, a horse-powered gristmill, and a theater. Most imposing of all was the two-story "La Grande Maison," supposedly built for the Queen. Life at the settlement was often similar to that at home, despite wilderness discomforts. There was time for boating, picnicking, and dinners in honor of such visiting notables as Louis Philippe, who later became King of France.

The exiled French, however, yearned for European civilization and dearly missed friends and relatives in France. Furthermore, financial difficulties and land disputes arose, and hostilities developed with neighboring Yankee settlers. When Napolean Bonaparte granted amnesty, many returned to France, but a few scattered to other parts of Pennsylvania. By the mid-1800s, Azilum was little more than another field along the winding Susquehanna.

0.0 (0.0) *Intersection of PA 187 and US 6 in Wysox; head south on PA 187.*

WYSOX is a grimy town sprawled out along busy US 6, with a dusty Masonite plant nearby. Two diners cater to farmers, truckers, and factory workers. Fulmer's Shopping Center, the large cross-shaped building at this intersection, is the former Piolett Mansion, built in 1872 and based on plans for a courthouse at French Azilum. The once-elegant home has lost most of its fine features (including an octagonal cupola) during years of neglect and its

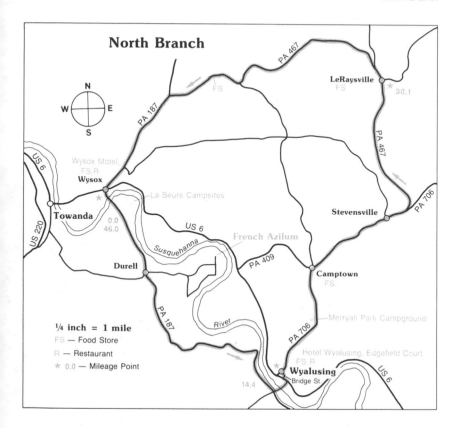

North Branch

¼ inch = 1 mile
FS — Food Store
R — Restaurant
* 0.0 — Mileage Point

conversion to a store and gas station.

PA 187 passes through river-bottom farmland before the terrain becomes slightly hillier and more wooded.

3.6 (3.6) *Durell; go straight on PA 187.*

> Left from Durell 3.9 miles on an unmarked road is the site of FRENCH AZILUM (717-265-3376). Now a state historic site, it consists of several reconstructed log cabins and a nineteenth-century farmhouse, all holding relics of the settlement.

Related to French Azilum is the story of the Pools, a group of people still inhabiting this area. They trace their ancestry to Anthony Vanderpool and several of his relatives, who came from New York's Mohawk Valley to work for the struggling French. Vanderpool had been disowned by his prominent Dutch family for marrying a half-breed woman, a daughter of Sir William Johnson, envoy to the Indians and a leading figure in the French and Indian War. After the Pools settled at nearby Pool Hill, they are said to have taken in black slaves who escaped from the French, adding to the clan's racial mixture. Pools typically have dark complexions, high cheekbones, and straight black hair.

Known as natural woodsmen, the Pools were capable of finding game, fish, and wild berries where others failed. They were also known as stupid, shiftless, untrustworthy, and malicious—a reputation which, often unfairly, haunts their descendants to this day. Area children still use "Pool" as a taunting name.

13.0 (9.4) *Intersection with an unmarked road; turn left and immediately cross a Susquehanna River bridge.*

13.8 (0.8) *Junction with US 6; turn left, then after 0.4 mile turn right on Bridge Street into Wyalusing.*

WYALUSING, located on a shelf above Wyalusing Creek, is a community with a pleasant small-town character. Its center looks like Main Street U.S.A., with Italianate two-story business buildings and much gingerbread ornamentation. It is a thriving town, with a variety of businesses. During the day it bustles as store owners set out items on the sidewalk, farmers stand on the corners talking, and wives arrive for shopping; at night the streets become vacant and quiet. Everybody seems to know everyone else.

In 1978 Wyalusing received national attention when a vision of Christ's face appeared on the tabernacle cloth of St. Mary of the Assumption Church. The miracle drew thousands of visitors; some walked away convinced, others saw nothing. Eventually the crowds' disruptions forced the priest to remove the cloth.

View of Wyalusing Creek at Camptown.

The Hotel Wyalusing (717-746-1204), with an ornate "showboat" front, is an early tavern that was enlarged over the years. The owners, two of Wyalusing's energetic businessmen, have remodeled its dining room, exposing the beams of the earlier structure, reinstalling original booths with unusual folding seats, and keeping a stone fireplace that has an alcove containing a lighted waterfall. The hotel has modern guest rooms with baths, as well as older, plainer rooms.

14.4 (0.6) *Intersection with PA 706 in Wyalusing; turn right.*

From Wyalusing through a fertile valley to Camptown, PA 706 follows the course of the Camptown Races, the horse races made famous by Stephen Foster. During the 1840s Foster attended school in nearby Towanda. With friends he often visited the popular race, which covered the five miles between the two towns. Local residents brought their best horses, used to pulling family carriages or plowing fields. Years afterward Foster remembered the fun and excitement of the races and wrote the now-familiar song.

17.2 Merryall Park Campground (May–Oct., 717-746-1243), situated along Wyalusing Creek, offers showers, a snack bar, and a swimming pool.

19.4 CAMPTOWN is a peaceful village of frame houses on Wyalusing Creek. The community celebrates Camptown Races Day on the second Saturday of September with a foot race, food, and entertainment.

Two house styles brought to northeastern Pennsylvania by Yankee settlers are evident in this valley. The classic cottage, or one-and-a-half, style is a descendent of the Cape Cod house, but it differs by having a shallower pitched roof, a higher loft which allows small rectangular windows under the eaves, and gable-end flues for stoves instead of a central chimney.

The second house style, which also appeared during the first half of the nineteenth century, is the Greek Revival temple. During this period New Englanders were fascinated by ancient Greece, and they manifested that interest in their architecture. This style is characterized by a door in the gable end, and also by Classical features such as pediment-like gables and pillar-like corners (called pilasters). Often one or two wings (sometimes of the older one-and-a-half design) are attached to the sides of the temple house, giving it the name, "upright and wing."

24.1 (9.7) *Turn left onto PA 467.*

The road begins a gradual climb among the rolling glacial hills through hay fields and wood lots, past farmsteads with frame houses and unpainted barns.

25.9 A slate quarry in the hillside on the left-hand side of the road shows that the rock layers of the Appalachian Plateau, an area left relatively undisturbed by the building of the Appalachian Mountains, are flat-lying.

26.8 Edsel's Sugar Cabin is one of many maple syrup producers in this part of the state.

30.1 LERAYSVILLE is a pleasant farming village with noticeable New England characteristics including a Greek Revival church, a gazebo on a green, and much white-painted clapboard architecture. The town was the site of a commune founded by the LeRaysville Phalanx, an association based on the principles of Charles Fourier. The commune failed after only eighteen months.

The LeRaysville Phalanx was one of hundreds of communal settlements established in the United States during the middle of the nineteenth century. Although they differed in political and religious orientation, all believed that social change was achievable through the development of a single ideal community which would be duplicated throughout the country. An important common element of their designs was the creation of an ideal pastoral setting; some, in fact, intended to recreate the Garden of Eden. Most communards wanted self-sufficient settlements that complemented industry with agriculture.

30.8 (6.7) *"Y"; bear left on PA 467.*

A gravel road on the left leads 0.6 mile to the UPCOUNTRY CHEESE HOUSE (9–5, Mon.-Sat.). The Amish began settling here two decades ago, intending to produce drinking milk. State health regulations changed, requiring them to install modern bulk milk containers. This they would not do, so they went into cheese production, where milk cans are allowed. Delicious cheese made on location as well as cheese from other places is sold in the store.

37.8 (7.0) *Junction; turn right on PA 467.*

41.2 (3.4) *Junction with PA 187; turn left.*

PA 187 follows the flood plain of sycamore-lined Wysox Creek. Along this road are several fruit and vegetable stands which sell local produce during the warmer months.

46.0 (4.8) *Wysox.*

Bicycle Shops:
None on route. The nearest shop is in Athens.

Eastern Highlands

In this region the forest stretches for miles, rarely broken by fields, highways, or towns, climbing one rugged mountain after another, descending to narrow trout-filled creeks and broad canyon streams. The slow but intense building of the Appalachian Mountains only caused ripples in the plateau bedrock here. Yet the geologic distortion was enough to push up the tough rock layers that then resisted ages of erosion to cause a highlands region. The mountainous fingers forming the region's northeast border are impressions of the geologic ripples.

Despite their weakened condition this far south, the continental glaciers created a few spectacular features that endure today. The Grand Canyon of Pennsylvania was formed when glacial debris forced Pine Creek to carve out a new southerly route. The twenty-five waterfalls of Ricketts Glen are the result of Kitchen Creek's having to trace a new course over the Allegheny Front, the Highlands southern escarpment. There are also glacial lakes, such as the one at Eagles Mere, an attractive resort in Sullivan County.

One hundred years ago this region was called the Black Forest because of its dark hemlock and white pine cover. The mountains were extensively logged, then abandoned. Brush fires burned unchecked, killing softwood seedlings. Early in the twentieth century, partly to prevent further devastation and partly because the land was cheap, the state began buying vast acreages. Today half of the Highlands—now mostly hardwood forest—is protected as state forest, state game land, or state park land.

The few villages and hamlets of the Highlands typically sit along streams with mountains looming overhead, and consist of simple frame buildings including a general store and a hotel. Most towns flourished during the logging days, but now they benefit from campers, fishermen, and hunters who come to enjoy the forested mountains.

The splendid wild scenery of the Highlands, the possibility of seeing bear, deer, and other wildlife, and the many opportunities to fish make bicycle touring here especially nature-oriented. Riding is fairly easy along the larger streams or on flat mountaintops, but the terrain between can be strenuous. Roads are few, but even the state highways have little traffic. There are many campgrounds and interesting old hotels, and primitive camping is allowed in the state forest land which borders many roadsides.

For More Information:

Clinton County Tourist Promotion Agency, Court House, Eastwater and Jay Streets, Lock Haven, PA 17745, (717) 893-4037

Endless Mountains Association (Bradford, Susquehanna, and Sullivan Counties), R.D. 6, Box 132A, Tunkhannock, PA 18657, (717) 836-5431

Lycoming County Tourist and Convention Bureau, 848 West Fourth Street, Williamsport, PA 17701, (800) 358-9900

Potter County Recreation, P.O. Box 245, Coudersport, PA 16915, (814) 435-2394

Tioga Association for Recreation and Tourism, P.O. Box 56, Mansfield, PA 16933, (800) 332-6718

Area Bicycle Club:

Williamsport Bicycle Club, 327 Adams Street, Williamsport, PA 17701

View of Pine Creek Valley from an overlook on the Black Forest Trail.

24 Sullivan Highlands

- **Sullivan County**
- **Start and end at Worlds End State Park**
- **21.5 miles; flat to rolling with one climb**
- **1 day**

About the time of the Civil War, Peter Armstrong, a Philadelphia rag collector and tinware merchant, inched his wagon full of clanging pots and pans up the steep mountain road that led into Sullivan County. A deeply religious man, he believed in the imminent return of Christ. Upon seeing the mountain woodlands and cool glens of the Sullivan Highlands, he decided that here he would establish Celestia—the Heavenly Celestial City—a community where all would share equally and where the Redeemer would return to live.

Armstrong, a man of indefatigable zeal, set about creating a settlement in the wilderness, alluring devotees through newspapers published in Philadelphia and Celestia, and urging the state legislature to classify Celestia's inhabitants peaceable aliens in wilderness exile. In 1864 he deeded the land and buildings to the inevitable heir, "Almighty God."

God, however, does not pay taxes. Consequently, the sheriff of Sullivan County sold the property, and Armstrong and his colonists returned to Philadelphia. Soon the community's several crude buildings succumbed to the surrounding forest and Celestia became only a memory.

0.0 (0.0) *Leaving the entrance to Worlds End State Park, turn left towards Laporte on PA 154.*

Located in a wooded canyon, WORLDS END STATE PARK (717-924-3287) was named for the precarious position of an early road on a nearby rocky mountainside, where travelers thought their lives were threatened. Here the rushing Loyalsock Creek makes a loop and quiets for a moment in an eddy beneath a hemlock-covered slope. During the 1930s the Civilian Conservation Corps, a Federal jobs program, dammed the eddy to make a swimming pool and built pavilions, rental cabins, and a campground nearby. Reservations are taken for cabins, but not for campsites.

Right from Worlds End State Park on PA 154 for 2.2 miles is FORKSVILLE, a picturesque village of frame houses, a general store, and a red covered bridge. Lodging, food, and beverages are available at Gardener's Inn (717-924-3251), 2.0 miles south of Forksville on PA 87.

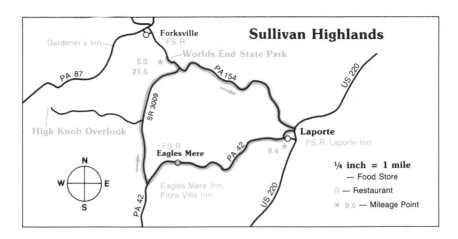

PA 154 follows along rocky Loyalsock Creek, its shores bordered by thick forest and fern-covered cliffs; then the road climbs through a wooded hollow.

7.7 (7.7) *Junction with US 220; turn right, then immediately right again.*

8.4 (0.7) *Junction with PA 42; turn right.*

Left on PA 42 a short distance is the business section of LAPORTE, a small county seat and resort surrounded by forest. When Sullivan County was created in 1847, the commissioners chose this central (though then unpopulated) location as the seat of government and hired the owner of the land, Michael Meylert, to build a town. Meylert was a colorful personage of some three hundred pounds, billed by one travel writer as a major area attraction. He was reputed to have killed a horse a year with fast driving, and his efforts at brick making resulted in both his home and the first courthouse's crumbling after a short period. But his devotion to the town matched his great size. Still evident are the maples that he and his wife planted along the streets and in the park and courthouse green which he planned for the community.

The Sullivan County Historical Museum (717–482–2311), in a small building behind the Courthouse, holds Peter Armstrong's famous deed, along with other relics of the area. Another attraction in town is the Laporte Little Theatre, with summer productions in the old Mokoma Inn.

The village itself is interesting for its Richardsonian Romanesque courthouse with brick and stone construction, tower, and arched windows and doorways; its shaded park with a pillory (for photographs only); and its numerous frame buildings with gable ends facing front in the New England style. (Meylert grew up among Connecticut Yankees in northeastern Pennsylvania.) Lake Mokoma, on the other side of US 220, belongs to a land association which allows public use of its beach for a charge.

9.9 The small lake in the woods on the left is Celestial Lake, the site of Peter Armstrong's Celestia and now uninhabited.

PA 42 crosses a slightly rolling mountaintop terrain through unbroken woodlands.

13.8 (5.4) *Eagles Mere; go straight on PA 42.*

The Indians believed that EAGLES MERE LAKE was once a great abyss where souls passed into the afterlife. One belligerent and malcontented chief known as Stormy Torrent decided to do the forbidden: to enter this chasm, converse with the ghosts of his ancestors, and then return with divine wisdom. On the appointed day, as thousands watched, Stormy Torrent descended a long flight of steps, accompanied by a beautiful princess from the shores of

Eagles Mere Inn.

Lake Erie. When they disappeared from view, the heavens darkened, blades of lightning struck nearby trees, and deafening thunder rolled across the mountain. An awful downpour followed, which filled the abyss to form a lake.

The lake actually was formed when the receding glacier dumped stones, sand, and earth it had accumulated farther north. The material blocked a stream valley, damming a lake. The sand brought the first settler, named Lewis, who operated a glass factory here. It now makes a fine beach.

At the turn of the century, EAGLES MERE was a thriving resort with numerous stately summer homes and three massive hotels. A narrow-gauge railroad offered station stops at each end of the lake and connected with Pullman coaches and sleepers making daily trips from Philadelphia. Although Eagles Mere is not a large lake, a small steam boat carried happy crowds across its placid waters.

The hotels, railroad, and steam boat are gone now, but wealthy Philadelphia families still spend their summers in the cedar shingle mansions of their grandparents. Eagles Mere has preserved its Victorian character and promotes itself as the "Gaslight Village." Several quaint shops, including a general store and an ice cream parlor, are near a small park with a gazebo. An ornate town clock stands near the general store. The Eagles Mere Inn (717-525-3273) is a fine country inn with an excellent menu and Saturday night entertainment.

15.0 (1.2) *Turn right onto the road to Worlds End (SR 3009).*

   17.5 A road to High Knob joins on the left.

   On this gentle paved forest road 4.8 miles is HIGH KNOB OVERLOOK, with a vista of seven counties. The picnic area and overlook were built by the C.C.C. on a mountain spur high above the Loyalsock Valley.

20.8 (5.8) *Junction with PA 154; turn left.*

21.5 (0.7) *Worlds End State Park.*

Bicycle Shops:
None on route. The nearest shop is in Williamsport.

25 Pine Creek

- **Lycoming and Tioga Counties**
- **Start and end at Little Pine State Park**
- **69.6 miles; flat to rolling with one climb**
- **2 days; overnight stop at Cedar Run Inn (mile 24.6),
  Pettecote Junction Camping Park (mile 24.6),
  or Blackwell Hotel (mile 30.4)**

In 1792 Charles Williamson, an agent for a wealthy landowner in England, faced the problem of getting settlers from Northumberland at the forks of the Susquehanna to his employer's tract in western New York State. A lengthy and dangerous route following the North Branch of the Susquehanna would normally have been taken, but the enterprising Williamson chose instead to build a direct road from the West Branch through wilderness to the northern border of the state.

To build the road Williamson enlisted the first set of English immigrants headed for New York State. All were unfamiliar with wilderness life and had to be trained in tree felling and road building. Often hardships made the crew rebellious, but Williamson, a man of indomitable perseverance, maintained order and completed the project in four years.

Williamson was so elated with his success he decided to hold a jubilee at his New York settlement—a bold proposal, considering its remote location. Handbills and circulars were sent throughout the mid-Atlantic states, where they were read in the national and state capitols and talked about widely among the general populace. For weeks before the festivities the Williamson Road, as well as other routes to Williamson's home, saw a procession of lively ladies and gentlemen, some accompanied by servants. The party was a time of horse-racing, plays, and general merrymaking, truly a success for Williamson and, indeed, a major influence in the settlement of this newly-opened region.

0.0 (0.0) *Leaving the park office at Little Pine State Park, turn right towards Waterville on SR 4001.*

LITTLE PINE STATE PARK (717-847-3209) has an oblong manmade lake enclosed by wooded mountainsides. There is a swimming area on the lake and a campground along the outlet. Campground reservations are accepted.

4.3 (4.3) *Junction with PA 44 in Waterville; turn right.*

WATERVILLE, at the confluence of Pine and Little Pine Creeks,

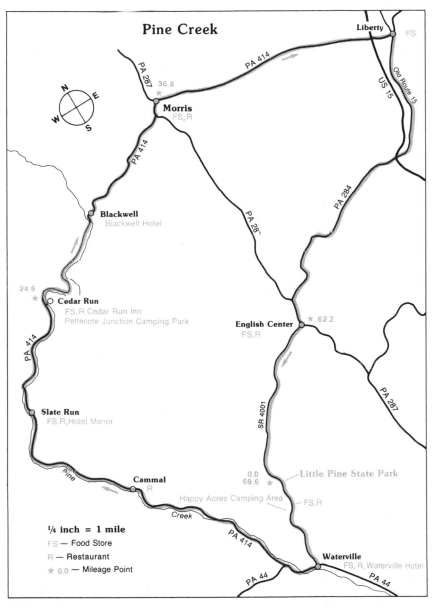

has a hotel and a general store as well as a few other businesses.
The Waterville Hotel (717-753-8231), a large frame building with a
second story porch, is a popular lodging for hunters. It has a bunk
room, plain rooms without baths, and a busy bar and restaurant—
the gathering place for the Waterville crowd.

5.9 (1.6) *Turn right onto PA 414.*

PA 414 follows Pine Creek Gorge, the Grand Canyon of Pennsylvania. Angular wooded mountains rise steeply 1,500 feet above the narrow valley floor. The headwaters of Pine Creek drained northward until, about 20,000 years ago, the continental ice sheet covered the area. When the ice sheet receded it left behind rock, sand, and clay which blocked Pine Creek's former course and sent it to carve out this new route.

A lightly traveled road, PA 414 passes through occasional cottage settlements and rustic villages. It is never far from wild Pine Creek, a popular rafting stream.

24.2 The little Baptist church on the left, alone except for a nearby farm, has pointed-top windows of the carpenter Gothic style. A local carpenter made these to imitate the arched windows of more elaborate Gothic churches.

24.6 A road to Cedar Run joins on the right.

> On this road 0.3 mile is CEDAR RUN, a pretty village of old frame buildings surrounded by wooded mountains. The Cedar Run Inn (717-353-6241), a turn-of-the-century hotel, is known for its period decor, fine food, and excellent wine list. Its rooms are comfortable, though not fancy. A wood stove warms the sitting room.
>
> Pettecote Junction Camping Park (717-353-7183) is along Pine Creek, where swimming is possible. It has showers.

After Cedar Run, PA 414 turns into a dirt road—one of only a few state routes to do that. The area is remote and pristine. Where the road climbs along a steep mountainside, there are views of Pine Creek rushing through a wooded canyon.

30.4 Pavement returns at BLACKWELL, a village set on a rise between Pine and Babb Creeks. Gable ends of many frame houses face the street, typical of Highlands communities. The Blackwell

View from the breast of Little Pine Creek Dam in Little Pine State Park.

Hotel (717-353-7435), has a restaurant and a bar and offers simple lodging.

The route continues on PA 414 through forest and along Babb Creek.

36.1 (30.2) *Junction with PA 287; turn left.*

36.8 (0.7) *Junction in Morris; turn right on PA 414.*

Now a run-down town spread out along PA 287, MORRIS blossomed in the late 1800s when one of the world's largest sole leather tanneries operated there. The works used ample local hemlock bark in the treatment of hides shipped in by rail. Morris was settled in 1800 by sawmill-owner Samson Babb, whose cabin has been restored and placed in a corner of the community's park.

From Morris, PA 414 climbs to a plateau farming area similar to that of the Northeast Region, before descending to Blockhouse Creek.

47.2 (10.4) *Junction in Liberty; turn right onto Old Route 15 (unmarked).*

LIBERTY grew from one of the blockhouses Williamson built at intervals to hold provisions and protect his crew's wives and children. When the road was finished, a Mr. Anthony, a veteran of the French Revolution and a particularly nasty character, converted the log blockhouse into a tavern. Anthony is said to have maintained a hidden pasture which tended to attract his overnight guests' cattle. In the morning the owners would wake to find their stock gone. Anthony would offer to search (forgetting the pasture), and the guests would leave heartbroken.

Old Route 15, tracing the Williamson Road, passes through a lightly farmed valley.

52.7 (5.5) *After passing under US 15, go straight onto PA 284.*

PA 284 descends gradually along Blockhouse Creek through a fairly unpopulated, thickly wooded area.

61.1 (8.4) *Junction with PA 287; turn left.*

62.2 (1.1) *English Center; turn right onto the road to Waterville.*

Passing meadows and streamside groves of sycamore, the road continues down along Little Pine Creek on a broader valley floor, with rugged mountains rising steeply all around.

69.6 (7.4) *Little Pine State Park.*

Bicycle Shops:
None on route. The nearest shops are in Wellsboro and Williamsport.

Appendix

MORE INFORMATION ON EASTERN PENNSYLVANIA

Bicycle Touring:

Bicycling Federation of Pennsylvania, 413 Appletree Road, Camp Hill, PA 17011. A state-wide organization of clubs and individuals, the Bicycling Federation of Pennsylvania offers a newsletter, information services, and an annual rally.

Harold Nanovic, Bicycle Coordinator, Pennsylvania Department of Transportation, Program Center, 917 Transportation and Safety Building, Harrisburg, PA 17120.

PennDOT Sales Store, Pennsylvania Department of Transportation, P.O. Box 2028, Harrisburg, PA 17105. Sells the *Pennsylvania Bicycling Guide,* which includes a free state map and four quadrant maps, each $1.25 postage paid. Pennsylvania residents should add six percent sales tax. The quadrant maps show hostels, restaurants, motels, repair shops, and campgrounds.

Travel:

Bureau of Travel Development, Pennsylvania Department of Commerce, 416 Forum Building, Harrisburg, PA 17120. Provides typical state tourist information.

Office of Public Information, Department of Environmental Resources, Box 2063, Harrisburg, PA 17120. Will send on request the *Pennsylvania Trail Guide*, a state map showing the location of various kinds of trails, including bicycle routes; and the *Pennsylvania Recreation Guide*, a state map showing the location of state parks, state forests, and state game lands. This map is useful in planning long distance tours.

Office of Public Information, Pennsylvania Historical and Museum Commission, Box 1026, Harrisburg, PA 17120. They are a source for information on museums and historic sites throughout the state, including a map of state historic properties.

General Maps:

Office of Public Information, Pennsylvania Department of Transportation, Transportation and Safety Building, Harrisburg, PA 17120. Distributes free copies of the official state map, which is useful in planning long-distance trips.

Publication Sales Store, Pennsylvania Department of Transportation, P.O. Box 2028, Harrisburg, PA 17105. Sells county road and traffic volume maps.

USGS, Map Distribution Branch, Box 25286, Denver Federal Center, Denver, CO 80255. Sells topographic maps in several scales. The 1:250,000 scale (one inch equals four miles) map is useful in planning long tours.

Franklin Survey Company, 1201 Race Street, Philadelphia, PA 19107. Sells southeastern Pennsylvania maps. Especially useful is the *Greater Delaware Valley USA* map.

Alfred B. Patton, 4143 Swamp Road, Doylestown, PA 18901. Sells a variety of county and regional maps for Pennsylvania.

MORE INFORMATION ON BICYCLE TOURING

Organizations:

League of American Wheelmen, Suite 209, 6707 Whitestone Road, Baltimore, MD 21207. Founded in 1880 and the oldest national organization of bicyclists, L.A.W. has a nationwide membership of clubs and individuals. Besides offering route information and listing of members who house bicyclists, the league pursues a vigorous legislative program, sponsors national rallies and publishes *BICYCLE USA* magazine and the *BICYCLE USA* Almanac.

Bikecentennial, P.O. Box 8308, Missoula, MT 59807. A bicycle touring organization, Bikecentennial has developed a number of routes, including the TransAmerica Trail, for which it has excellent guides. *The Cyclist's Yellow Pages* is the most complete listing of maps, books, organizations, and group tours across the country.

American Youth Hostels, Inc., National Office, P.O. Box 37613, Washington, DC 20013. Operates a system of hostels across the country and organizes outdoor trips, including bicycle touring.

Publications:

Bicycling, 33 East Minor Street, Emmaus, PA 18048. A monthly publication dedicated to all aspects of bicycling.

Effective Cycling, John Forrester, 1983, MIT Press (Cambridge, MA). A complete presentation of safe bicycling techniques, the recommended text for the League of American Wheelmen's Effective Cycling course.

Delong's Guide to Bicycles and Bicycling, Fred Delong, 1978, Chilton Book Company (Radnor, PA). A thorough book covering maintenance, repair, riding technique, health, and clothing.

Anybody's Bike Book, Tom Cuthbertson, 1979, Ten Speed Press (Berkley, CA). A light-hearted, nontechnical approach to bicycle maintenance and repair.

The Bicycle Touring Book, Tim and Glenda Wilhelm, 1980, Rodale Press (Emmaus, PA). A good basic how-to book for the would-be bicycle tourist.

Bike Touring: The Sierra Club Guide to Outings on Wheels, Raymond Bridge, 1979, Sierra Club (San Francisco, CA). Covers all aspects of bicycle touring from selecting a bicycle to clothing, safety, and low impact camping.

BICYCLE TOURING CHECKLIST

Clothing: bike shoes, regular shoes, socks, spare underwear, riding shorts, bathing suit, slacks, long-sleeved shirt(s), jersey(s), sweater and/or down vest, warm-up suit, windbreaker, riding gloves, helmet, rainwear.

Body Care: Band-Aids, gauze, adhesive tape, tweezers, hydrogen peroxide, Tylenol, sunscreen lotion, toiletries, insect repellent, sun glasses.

Maintenance: 6-inch crescent wrench, needlenose pliers, freewheel remover, spoke wrench, chain tool, tire patch kit, tire irons, screwdriver, pump, Mafac wrench kit (metric), chain lube, bearing grease, cleaning rag, spare tube, extra spokes with nipples, extra cable, extra valve cores, extra chain links, extra nuts and bolts, sewing kit.

Camping: sleeping bag and waterproof sack, sleeping pad, camp stove and fuel bottle, mess kit, tent and groundsheet, matches in waterproof case, can opener, scouring pad and soap.

Miscellany: Water bottle, safety flag, camera, wallet, plastic bags, maps, flashlight, note pad and pencils, lock and chain, 30 feet of nylon cord, candle lantern, pant clips.

Guidebooks from The Countryman Press and Backcountry Publications

Written for people of all ages and experience, these popular and carefully prepared books feature detailed trail and tour directions, notes on points of interest and natural phenomena, maps and photographs.

Walks and Rambles Series

Walks and Rambles on the Delmarva Peninsula, $9.95
Walks and Rambles in Dutchess and Putnam Counties (NY), $9.95
Walks and Rambles in Rhode Island, $9.95
Walks and Rambles in the Upper Connecticut River Valley, $9.95
Walks and Rambles in Westchester (NY) and Fairfield (CT) Counties, $8.95

Biking Series

25 Mountain Bike Tours in Vermont, $9.95
25 Bicycle Tours on Delmarva, $8.95
25 Bicycle Tours in Eastern Pennsylvania, $8.95
20 Bicycle Tours in the Finger Lakes, $8.95
20 Bicycle Tours in the 5 Boroughs (NYC), $8.95
25 Bicycle Tours in the Hudson Valley, $9.95
25 Bicycle Tours in Maine, $9.95
25 Bicycle Tours in New Hampshire, $7.95
25 Bicycle Tours in New Jersey, $8.95
20 Bicycle Tours in and around New York City, $7.95
25 Bicycle Tours in Ohio's Western Reserve, $9.95
25 Bicycle Tours in Vermont, $8.95

Canoeing Series

Canoe Camping Vermont and New Hampshire Rivers, $7.95
Canoeing Central New York, $10.95
Canoeing Massachusetts, Rhode Island and Connecticut, $7.95

Hiking Series

50 Hikes in the Adirondacks, $11.95
50 Hikes in Central New York, $9.95
50 Hikes in Central Pennsylvania, $9.95
50 Hikes in Eastern Pennsylvania, $10.95
50 Hikes in the Hudson Valley, $10.95
50 Hikes in Massachusetts, $11.95
50 More Hikes in New Hampshire, $9.95
50 Hikes in New Jersey, $10.95
50 Hikes in Northern Maine, $10.95
50 Hikes in Ohio, $12.95
50 Hikes in Southern Maine, $10.95
50 Hikes in Vermont, $11.95
50 Hikes in West Virginia, $9.95
50 Hikes in Western New York, $11.95
50 Hikes in Western Pennsylvania, $11.95
50 Hikes in the White Mountains, $12.95

Adirondack Series

Discover the Adirondack High Peaks, $14.95
Discover the Central Adirondacks, $8.95
Discover the Eastern Adirondacks, $9.95
Discover the Northeastern Adirondacks, $9.95
Discover the Northern Adirondacks, $10.95
Discover the Northwestern Adirondacks, $12.95
Discover the South Central Adirondacks, $10.95
Discover the Southeastern Adirondacks, $9.95
Discover the Southern Adirondacks, $10.95
Discover the Southwestern Adirondacks, $9.95
Discover the West Central Adirondacks, $13.95

Ski-Touring Series

25 Ski Tours in Central New York, $8.95
25 Ski Tours in New Hampshire, $8.95

Other Guides

Maine: An Explorer's Guide, $14.95
New England's Special Places, $12.95
New Jersey's Special Places, $12.95
New York State's Special Places, $12.95
Pennsylvania Trout Streams and their Hatches, $14.95
State Parks and Campgrounds in Northern New York, $9.95
Vermont: An Explorer's Guide, $16.95
Waterfalls of the White Mountains, $14.95

The above titles are available at bookstores and at certain sporting goods stores or may be ordered directly from the publisher. For complete descriptions of these and other guides, write: The Countryman Press, P.O. Box 175, Woodstock, VT 05091.